Mabel Hubbard Bell

A Biography

by

Ann J. Bishundayal

PROTEA PUBLISHING

Mabel Hubbard. A Biography.
Ann J. Bishundayal

ISBN 1-883707-71-4   soft cover

ISBN 1-931768-23-4   hardcover

First Edition Worldwide

Library Of Congress Control Number: 00-111478

Protea Publishing Company. USA

email:kaolink@msn.com

web site:www.proteapublishing.com

This book is dedicated to my children:

Beverlee Bishundayal

Stephanie Bishundayal

Jaclyn Bishundayal

and

Samantha Bishundayal

As the song goes,
"You're the best thing that ever happened to me."

Contents

Introduction

Early Views of Mabel Hubbard
Contained In The US Library 0f Congress
Circa 1905.

Important Dates

Original short article that inspired this book
"Further Contributions To The Study Of That Subtile Art
Which May Inable One With An Observant Eie To Heare What
Any Man Speaks By The Moving Of The Lips." (Bulwer 1648)
A paper written by Mrs. Alexander Graham Bell, July, 1894.

References

Bibliography

Picture Credits

Acknowledgements

Thanks

Introduction

*W*hen my eldest daughter, Beverlee, first entered Kindergarten in the fall of 1986, I as a parent was warmly welcomed to her school by parent volunteers. Those parents were members of the local Home & School Association at Elizabeth Ballantyne School in Montreal West. For me it was a wonderful introduction to my daughters' school and the beginning of my own involvement as a parent volunteer with the Home & School Association.

As sisters Stephanie, Jaclyn & Samantha joined Beverlee my involvement became more intense. In 1991 I became President of the local Home and School Association at Elizabeth Ballantyne School and held that post for four years. For three of those years (1992-1995), I was a con-current provincial Vice-President with the Quebec Federation of Home and Schools Association (QFHSA).

In 1995 our national organization, the Canadian Home & School, Parent-Teacher Federation (CHSPTF), now called the Canadian Home & School Federation (CHSF), celebrated it's 100th Anniversary. I wanted to make a special contribution to that event and so decided to write a short article on our founder, Mabel Hubbard. I published this short story in my own local school Newsletter, The EB Update. Subsequently the provincial newspaper for the QFHSA, NEWS, carried it as a front page story. Through some exhaustive research I discovered that Mabel Hubbard was a rather remarkable woman. Her life story inspired me to expand on my short article and this book is a result of that inspiration.

I learnt that there was so much more to this woman pioneer than merely the founder of the Canadian Home & School. This remarkable deaf woman who became the wife of Alexander Graham Bell and an honorary member of the Telephone Pioneers of America made valuable and long-lasting contributions to both the Canadian and American communities in which she lived.

I hope you will enjoy reading this book as much as I enjoyed writing it. It truly was a labour of love and I hope you too will discover and take delight in the remarkable life of Mabel Hubbard.

Ann J. Bishundayal

Early Views of Mabel Hubbard

Contained In The US Library Of Congress

Circa 1905

Part I

Mabel's Life 1857 – 1923

1 Year old Mabel with her mother
Gertrude McCurdy Hubbard
Cambridge, Mass. 1858

1. *Growing Up In Cambridge*

Mabel Hubbard was born on November 25th, 1857 in Cambridge, Massachusetts, USA. Her parents Gertrude McCurdy and Gardiner Greene Hubbard had five daughters altogether - Gertrude, Mabel, Roberta, Grace and Marian. They were a wealthy family living on Brattle Street in Cambridge, a city that Mabel's father had helped found years earlier in 1846.

Gardiner Greene Hubbard was a lawyer by profession and a well-known businessman in the community. His wealth afforded him the influence to make things happen in Cambridge and his commitment to the community helped make it into a thriving city. He accomplished much for the community together with other local businessmen and was often described as a man of great initiative, with a keen and active interest in movements for the public welfare. Together, Gardiner Greene Hubbard and other local businessmen, formed the Cambridge Water Works in 1852, along with the Gas Light Company, and also in 1852 the Cambridge Railroad. A man of great foresight, he was always looking for ways to improve the way of life for people in the community and whether it was recognizing the need for street snow removal or getting new streets built, Mr. Hubbard was at the forefront of the new improvements. This sense of caring and commitment was something he passed on to his daughter Mabel.

Mabel, or "May", as she was often called had a happy childhood and was described as a stunning girl with gray/blue eyes and light brown hair. She was full of life, artistic, curious and eager to learn. At the age of five, in 1863, she contracted Scarlet Fever after a visit to her grandparent's home in New York. The disease left Mabel deaf and this of course also affected her balance. It was a terrible blow for the family. Luckily she had the kind of parents who cared enough to seek help for their daughter. In those Victorian days such a person as Mabel would have been called "insane" and segregated from society - often they were institutionalized. This was not Mabel's fate as her parents did not associate deafness with insanity.

The Hubbards sought out all the information they could on how to educate a deaf child. They did not want their child to live in a world of silence and isolation. Mr. Hubbard, who at that time happened to be a member of the Massachusetts State Board of Education, was able to find a school in Germany that had developed a way to preserve the speech of deaf children. In a report written by teachers Dr. Samuel Howe and Horace Mann, the Hubbards learnt of German deaf children, who spoke and understood what others were saying by reading their lips. Dr. Howe encouraged Mabel to talk and so began a remarkable journey for Mabel Hubbard. It wasn't going to be an easy one but Mabel was up for the challenge. May was a tenacious young girl and nothing was going to hold her back from leading a normal life.

Everyone in the Hubbard household was instructed to speak to Mabel as if she could hear. They were told to ignore any signs she might make and literally "force" her to speak! Despite the lack of help and encouragement from professionals of the day who worked with deaf children, Mabel learnt to read lips. In 1864, to help further her development, a governess by the name of Miss Conklin, was brought into the Hubbard home to teach Mabel to read. That was not such a hard task to accomplish as Mabel just adored books and read anything and everything she could get her hands on. Her father had an extensive library full of historical works and Mabel just read one book after another. She wasn't one for playing outdoors like the other children but preferred to curl up with a good book indoors. Her love for the great outdoors would develop later in life. Things were going well for Mabel. Her spectacular success in speaking and reading proved all the experts wrong.

In the summer of 1865 the Hubbard home was having extensive repairs and renovations done so the entire family packed up and went to Bethel, Maine for the summer. There they stayed at the home of Dr. Nathanial P. True. That summer Mabel and Dr. True's daughter, Mary, became friends and eventually her teacher. Mary True had just become trained as a teacher that summer and in the fall was invited to the Hubbards Cambridge home as Mabel's governess. She arrived there on October 24th, 1865. Mabel in later years described Mary True not only as her teacher but also as her "friend for all time".

Mr. Hubbard was still working hard for the rights of deaf children and in 1867 he successfully petitioned the Massachusetts Legislature, with the help of his daughter, Mabel. As a result the following two bills were enacted: -

1. To establish the Clarke Institute For Deaf Mutes at Northampton, Massachusetts, later called the Clarke School For The Deaf.

2. To provide teaching of deaf children 5-10 years old at the Clarke and other schools for deaf in the State of Massachusetts with funds to be provided by the State.

At those legislative hearings ten-year-old Mabel was the "star" witness and surprised and astonished everyone in attendance. There she was, a deaf child able to speak and answer any amount of questions thrown at her. Questions on all manner of subjects were asked of Mabel and she was able to answer them all. She proved herself to be intelligent beyond her years. Her father became the first president of the Clarke School For The Deaf and held that position for ten years (1867-1877). Mr. Hubbard always maintained an interest in the education of deaf children for the rest of his life and it was thanks to his persistence that the schools were established. Children at the deaf schools were then taught to lip-read and speak. Mr. Hubbard and Mabel had scored a major victory for the rights of deaf children.

That summer, however, proved to be both a joyful one as Mabel continued to show great progress in her lip reading and speaking skills and a sad one for the Hubbard family. While Mabel was in Bethel, Maine, her two-year-old sister, Marian, died in Cambridge. Infant mortality during Victorian times was common place due to various diseases, but it was never the less a great loss for Mabel, her parents and her sisters.

In the fall of 1869 Mabel and her sisters attended a private school called Miss Songer's School. Meanwhile Mary True became a teacher at the Horace Mann School For The Deaf, but continued to live with the Hubbards in their Brattle Street home. She was no longer Mabel's governess, but remained as Mabel's close friend. The following summer the Hubbard family took off to Europe where they lived and traveled for almost three years. Gardiner Greene Hubbard returned to Cambridge in the fall of

1871 because of business commitments and the rest of the family remained in Europe taking in all the many wonderful and varied sights.

Mabel and her sisters enjoyed quite an education whilst in Europe. Mabel attended a school in Vienna run by Herr and Frau Lehfeld and Miss Harriet Rogers, principal of the Clarke School was invited to stay with Mabel during that time to help her with her German. It was a learning experience for both of them, but the ever eager Mabel was reading German in no time! In fact Mabel became so proficient in German that she would be the one to take her parents shopping and sightseeing, translating for them and her sisters. It was obvious that this little deaf child, who had adapted to the hearing world so readily, was destined for greatness. She just stood out from the crowd, exuding her own personal aura. Meanwhile, Mrs. Hubbard and older sister Gertrude were living in Paris while sisters Berta and Grace attended a private school in Switzerland.

Mabel and her sisters had quite a privileged lifestyle. They visited Rome, Florence, Paris, England and always had teachers with them to explain the architecture, the arts, and the history of the places they visited. The world was their classroom and their education was not lacking at all. In Victorian times girls did not go off to college to further their education as the men did, but for the Hubbard girls' travelling was their education. Mabel was also a keen writer and sent letters constantly to her grandparents back in the United States describing in great detail all the wondrous sights that Europe had to offer. Mabel kept all her letters throughout her lifetime and it is through them that we are able to learn so much about her.

Mabel's father, Gardiner Greene Hubbard

Mabel's father, Gardiner Greene Hubbard

HARVARD BRANCH RAILROAD.

FOR CAMBRIDGE COLLEGES.

ON AND AFTER MONDAY, JAN. 5, 1852,

TRAINS WILL RUN AS FOLLOWS:

LEAVE CAMBRIDGE, NEAR THE COLLEGES,	LEAVE BOSTON, AT THE FITCHBURG STATION,
7.30 A. M.	8.00 A. M.
8.30 "	9.30 "
10.15 "	12.45 P. M.
1.40 P. M.	2.15 "
3.30 "	3.50 "
4.25 "	5.30 "
6.30 "	6.50 "
7.10 "	*11.15 "

* Except on Saturdays, when it will leave at 10 P. M.

NEW ARRANGEMENT.

Season Tickets, $6 per quarter. Package Tickets, ten for a dollar, will convey passengers from and to Cambridge to Dover Street, or to the New South Boston Bridge, by the Dover street Omnibus and the South Boston Omnibus, which leave the Fitchburg Station on the arrival of each train.

Tickets to and from Cambridge to Fitchburg Station at fifty cents for a package of seven. Single Tickets ten cents, for cars only. For sale at the Railroad Stations, and by Charles Stimpson, 103 Washington street, Boston.

Passengers taken to and from the Station in Cambridge to any distance now run by the Cambridge Omnibuses in the First Ward, for three cents. Order slate, at Wood & Hall's and at the Station.

The office in Boston is in the Lowell Ticket Office, Scolley's Buildings, Court street. Passengers called for at this Office.

PRINTED AT THE CAMBRIDGE

Schedule of the
Harvard Branch Railroad
1852

The Italianate Bracketed style Brattle Street home (#146) of the Hubbard Family.

Georgian Revival House(#146 Brattle Street)
Built in 1939

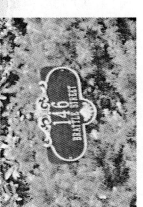

Georgian Revival House (#146 Brattle Street)
Built in 1939

18 Beacon Street – Bell's rooms around 1873 where Mabel had some of her lessons.

Hubbard Park Rd. street sign – only indication left that the Hubbard's once lived here.

Mabel in 1862 aged 4/5 (top)
At age 6 (reading) – self portrait 1875 (age 18)

Mabel at 14(top)
With sister Grace (at right)
Mabel loved to read.

Mabel always dressed with grace & elegance.

2. Enter Mr. Bell

*W*hile Mabel and her sisters were in Europe with mother, father, Gardiner Greene Hubbard was back in Boston attending to his business matters. Fate was now beginning to take a hand in Mabel's life. Mr. Hubbard was introduced to a teacher for the deaf by the name of Mr. Alexander Graham Bell (he was on the faculty of Boston University as professor of vocal physiology) - a young man from Scotland, who was living in Tutela Heights, Ontario, Canada with his parents, and newly arrived in the United States in April of 1871. Bell was teaching also at the Clarke Institute for Deaf Mutes that Hubbard had helped establish in 1867 and where he (Hubbard) was still the President.

Upon Mabel's return to Cambridge in 1873 Mary True introduced her to Mr. Bell. Mabel was now a slender, attractive sixteen year old girl with dark brown hair and very graceful in her manner. Mabel took an instant dislike to Mr. Bell and found him scruffy and scrawny. However fate played a hand again! Mr. Hubbard had taken a liking to Mr. Bell. He was impressed with this young teacher of the deaf and hired him as Mabel's private teacher. Mabel did not have many lessons with Mr. Bell. Mary True would take Mabel to her lessons but she was mostly taught by Mr. Bell's assistant, Abby Locke, with Mr. Bell offering suggestions and guidance from time to time. History has said that Mr. Bell was her only teacher but a letter that Mabel wrote in 1906 clarifies the matter, " I met Mr. Bell first when I was nearly sixteen. Miss True brought me to call on him at his offices in Boston University - I had a few lessons from him - and more from his assistant - but by that time my habits of speech were fixed and he could do little to change them in the short time I was under his instruction." [1] She further explained, "So for good or evil my acquirements as speaker and speech reader go back chiefly to my mother and Miss True." [2]

In that letter Mabel gives much credit to her mother and Miss True as her main influences and teachers but did add a postscript that read, " On further reflection I want to modify my statement a little. Mr. Bell did help me a good deal - he was too remarkable a teacher not to impress his mark on any pupil with whom he came into contact." [3] It seemed almost like a guilty afterthought that she had not given enough credit to her husband. Mabel did enjoy her lessons at Mr. Bell's offices and she would make the effort to go no matter what the weather conditions - even in the worst snowstorm!

In the meantime her father and Mr. Bell were becoming good friends because of their mutual interests in the deaf and also in telegraphy. In October of 1874 Mr. Bell was invited to tea at the Hubbard home and there after became a frequent visitor. Mabel still did not like this scraggy, scruffy looking man!

That same fall Mabel gave her first formal dance at the Hubbard home and from all accounts looked stunning in a beautiful peach silk gown. Mr. Bell was falling in love with Mabel and was also busy "inventing" for her father. Consequently he was a frequent visitor at the Hubbard home. That suited Mr. Bell well as he got to see a lot of his beloved Mabel and although she still didn't find him attractive she was interested in his scientific work and would often ask questions and offer suggestions. Bell was so taken with Mabel that he wrote a letter to her mother expressing his feelings - knowing Mabel did not yet feel the same way about him. Mrs. Hubbard replied telling Mr. Bell to give it time, wait another year and then see if he still felt the same way.

Mr. Bell did not give up. In the summer of 1875 he even followed Mabel to Nantucket where she was staying with her cousin Mary Blatchford. Mary told her all about Mr. Bell's letter and when he showed up at the front door Mabel refused to see him! Mabel did not love Mr. Bell. She decided to write him a letter to tell him so but also said that she would like to get better acquainted upon her return to Cambridge at the end of the summer. They did get a chance to talk privately one August night in the greenhouse of the Hubbard home and from then on their relationship blossomed. It must have been strange for any onlooker to see them converse under the lights of the greenhouse. Remember Mabel could only respond if she saw the other person's lips moving so she could read them! Bell was a happy man. He sensed that Mabel was taking a liking to him. Mabel, however, was still not in love with him at that time.

Bell went back to his parents Brantford home in Canada for the rest of the summer and returned to Cambridge in October not only to see Mabel but also with patent specifications for the telephone. He was still teaching at the Clarke Institute and pursued inventing on his own time - earning about $5,000 a year. Mabel's father was getting a little frustrated with Bell by then because he wanted him to give up teaching and concentrate on inventing and working on telegraphy and the telephone. Mr. Hubbard reminded Bell that working on his inventions with him would keep him closer to Mabel! Bell refused to give up teaching of the deaf as it was so dear to his heart.

By the fall of 1875 Mabel realized that she loved Bell, a man ten years her senior. On November 25th, 1875, Mabel's 18th birthday and coincidentally Thanksgiving Day, they were engaged. During their engagement Bell was very busy with his inventions and Mabel took a great interest in his work with both the multiple telegraph and the telephone. Mabel had always been curious and became fascinated with the scientific aspects of the telephone. She knew this invention was going to benefit mankind greatly once it was perfected. She and her father both could see a future for this thing called a telephone. Mabel and her father craftily steered Bell away from his "visible speech" work (the great joy of his life) and made him work long and hard on the telephone. Due to their persistence, one of the most valuable patents ever issued was registered in March of 1876 - United States Patent No. 174,465 - that of the basic telephone.

In 1876 Mr. Hubbard organized an educational exhibit in Philadelphia - "The Centennial Exhibition". Mabel and her father wanted Bell to show his telephone, but he was reluctant to go to the exhibition stating that he had an examination to give for the teachers of the deaf. Mabel tricked him into going, however, she got him on the train and packed all his instruments. She and her father believed in the "phone" and knew the rewards it could bring. While Bell was at work Mabel had gone to his rooms with her mother and packed his bag. Then she bought a train ticket and got money for him for the journey. Meanwhile she had persuaded Bell to go for a carriage ride with her and had told the coachman beforehand to take them straight to the train station. Once at the train station she told Bell to get on the train and that his assistant, Willie, was waiting for him with his bags, ticket and money. Bell still refused to go so Mabel resorted to tears and said that if he didn't go she wouldn't marry him. Mr. Bell boarded the train to Philadelphia!

It was a very hot Sunday in June - the 25th - and fate was about to take another hand. The judges were about to call it quits for the day on account of the heat, just before they reached Bell's exhibit. One of the judges was Emperor Don Pedro of Brazil, someone that Bell had met sometime earlier in Boston. He recognised Bell and persuaded the judges to take a look at his telephone. They were impressed and Bell received the highest award for the most interesting exhibit. Mabel upon hearing the news back in Cambridge was elated. She had faith and great belief in his telephone. Had she not forced him to go to the exhibit he may have given up on the phone as he was prone to give up on many inventions once he found something else to interest him. She knew him well. She knew also that he would be famous all over the world one day and she knew that his talents as an inventor would bring him "greatness". Throughout their engagement the two would write constantly to one another whenever they were apart even for the briefest of times. Even after Mabel had tricked Bell into going to Philadelphia he wrote her a very "loving" letter, " ...want merely to show you that I have not forgotten my dear little fiancée... if it should happen that there is more paper than writing in my letter to you - please believe me that I have a heart full of manuscript reserved for your special eye when fate permits me to return... My darling pet I miss you very much. How I wish I could only see you May if it was only for a moment! Your loving Alec." [4]   There was no doubt that Mabel and Alec were truly in love with one another.

Their engagement was about a year and a half long and during that time they did spend a great deal of time apart, due to Bell's work with the telephone, but they kept writing those love letters constantly to each other. It seemed that they could not bear to be apart so much. Towards the end of 1876 Mabel had the opportunity to travel across the United States by luxury private railway cars. Her father had been appointed by the President of the United States to chair a special commission to investigate the problem of transporting mail by rail. From Chicago, across the Prairies, to Salt Lake City, to Denver, she traveled. The sights were awesome and having undertaken such a journey myself (by Greyhound in the 70's) I can attest to the beauty and the excitement of it all. It must have been more spectacular in those days with less construction and more natural beauty to behold. Mabel wrote Bell many long letters along the way and explained in great detail all the sights she saw. The following year the two were wed.

The Cambridge Chronicle misspells Mr. Bell's name
in the marriage announcement
July 14th, 1877

57 West Cromwell Road, South Kensington, London England. Mabel's home from November 1877 – November 1878

Room in Greenock Academy used by A.G. Bell in 1878
for the Articulation School

In a room filled with the sweet smell of Madonna Lilies against the backdrop of crimson curtains, Mabel and Mr. Bell were married on July 11th, 1877. It was a beautiful sunny afternoon. The marriage announcement appeared in the local newspaper, The Cambridge Chronicle as follows on July 14th, 1877: -

BALL - HUBBARD - *In this city, 11th inst, by Rev. Alexander McKenzie, Alexander G. Ball, of Boston, and Mabel G. Hubbard of this city.*

Yes they had misspelled the name. Somehow the Ball Telephone just doesn't sound the same does it!

Bell's wedding gift to his beautiful bride was a cross of 11 round pearls and 1,507 shares in his new company, The Bell Telephone Company which had been founded only two days earlier on July 9th, 1877. Bell had also given Mabel another gift that year from his first earnings made from the telephone. He reportedly made about $149 and had a silver model of the basic telephone made for Mabel at a cost of $85. It was one of her most cherished possessions. Mabel and Bell had a traditional honeymoon at Niagara Falls and then went on to visit Bell's parents in Brantford, Ontario. This was Mabel's first meeting with Bell's parents and it would be one she would never forget. Before Mabel was allowed to enter the Bell home Mrs. Bell came out and broke oatcake over her head ! This was an old Scottish tradition ensuring that they would never go hungry - and they never did. The following evening a party was given in Mabel and Bell's honour. Invited guests included Members of Parliament, farmers and lawyers. That night at the party, Chief Johnson of the Six Nations spoke in Mohawk into Bell's telephone during a demonstration in the Bell home. It had been an exciting visit to Brantford for Mabel.

The happy couple returned to Boston and on August 4th, 1877 sailed from New York on the SS Anchoria to spend some time in Scotland and England. They docked at the beautiful town of Greenock, Scotland and then went on to Glasgow for a few days. Then it was all the way down to Plymouth where Bell had been invited to demonstrate his telephone. Bell gave many lectures during their first few months in England and Scotland. Despite Bell's pressing engagements the couple did take time for a second honeymoon. Bell took Mabel to visit his hometown of Edinburgh. He showed her his old home on Charlotte Square (still part of the official bus tour today!), then they went further north to Banff, Elgin and Covesea near Lossiemouth. It was during this time while staying at a fisherman's cottage at Covesea that Mabel discovered she was pregnant. Bell had thought that he and Mabel could rough it while living in the cottage and live off the land and sea. Mabel, on the other hand, was not too happy at the thought of catching, cleaning and cooking their own fish and persuaded him to let the landlady take care of the cooking. He agreed and the couple spent an enjoyable week at Covesea. Mabel had quite a talent for sketching and spent many an afternoon sitting on the rocks sketching while Bell would play around amongst the rocks his mind ever "inventing".

Before they left to go back to London Bell bought Mabel a pair of baby socks to celebrate the coming birth.

Once in London they took rooms in a private hotel on Jermyn Street - a street where Sir Isaac Newton had lived 150 years earlier. Bell was kept busy with lectures and his inventing and experimenting. Mabel kept busy writing his letters, keeping notes and translating German scientific articles for Bell. The space in the rooms was limited and Mabel soon became frustrated with the small rooms as they were beginning to fill up with endless mounds of papers and inventions. Bell liked to work late into the night and this was making Mabel very agitated. She needed more space - they needed more space!

Around November of 1877 they moved into a much larger home at 57 West Cromwell Road in South Kensington. This home had four floors, seventeen rooms, and a large garden with a yearly rent of £225. Mary Home who had been a housekeeper for Bell's grandfather joined the household and became a valuable member of the household staff. Mabel was feeling pangs of loneliness.

She was so used to having lots of people around as in their Brattle Street home in Cambridge, Massachusetts. Bell was gone frequently and it was sometimes frustrating and lonely for her. Sundays, however, did turn into the "happy" day of the week for Mabel as she and Bell would often invite guests over for the day.

It felt more like the Cambridge days for Mabel. Now, although Mabel was the one expecting, it was Mr. Bell who was putting on the pounds and growing whiskers too. Mabel remained slim and graceful until the latter part of her pregnancy but she was becoming concerned about Alec's weight increase.

Bell was still working late into the night (or should I say the wee hours of the morning) and it was very hard to get him out of bed in the mornings. This was a sore point throughout their married life, which in time Mabel just came to accept. A typical week for Mabel would be breakfast around 8.30 am with Bell. He would then spend his mornings in his lab or with his secretary. Mabel would read, do needlework, attended to household affairs and would dine with Bell around 7pm. They would spend the evenings together talking about the day's events and Bell's work. Mabel usually went to bed around 10 pm - Bell usually not before 1 am! On Sundays Bell would stay in bed until about 10 am and dinner would be at three with their invited guests. Mabel was still writing many letters to her parents, grandparents and sisters back in the United States keeping them informed on every occurrence in the Bell household - and there were many! An event that caused Mabel a fair amount of distress was when her husband was asked to give Queen Victoria a demonstration of his telephone. Mabel naturally assumed that she would be accompanying Alec to the palace for this great event and so set about ordering a special gown. She went to Paris and had several fittings for an exquisite black silk dress for the occasion only to be told at the last minute that Queen Victoria had not requested her presence! It was a great disappointment to Mabel. Was it because Mabel was deaf and her speaking voice was not like that of others? Would Queen Victoria have found her presence uncomfortable? No reasons were ever given.

Mabel's mother, Mrs. Hubbard, arrived in London in the spring of 1878 to be with Mabel for the birth of her first child. Elsie May was born on the evening of May 8th, 1878 and one of the first things Alec checked was that she could hear. Elsie's hearing was normal and she was a beautiful baby with an abundance of dark hair and bluish eyes. Mabel now faced another challenge as a deaf person. How does a deaf person hear their baby cry? As usual Mabel had a solution. She placed a drawer next to her bed filled with soft pillows for the baby to lay in and whenever the baby cried the vibrations from the drawer would awaken her.

Mabel always worried about money and by the late summer of 1878 noticed that money was getting "tight". Bell was not earning enough to support the three of them plus the home and all of its expenses. The public was no longer excited about the telephone and there was a lot of bad press starting to surface about Bell. The press was saying that he was a thief and dishonourable and that he had stolen the idea for the telephone! It upset Mabel greatly and even more so when Bell did not defend himself to the press. Bell was fed up with the telephone and was concentrating more on his interest of teaching deaf children.

In the meantime, some parents in Greenock, Scotland were in need of his expertise in teaching the deaf. They needed a school and a qualified teacher for their deaf children. In the fall of 1878 Bell went back to Greenock to help the children who were so very important to him. He wanted to make sure these children would have everything they needed. This angered Mabel, who at this time did not like Bell's involvement with the deaf. As a deaf woman herself this did seem odd but she wanted him to have nothing to do with teaching at all. Over the years this would all change but then it angered her no end. It appeared as if she was in denial of her own deafness.

Bell had received a letter from a parent of a deaf child, Mr. Thomas Borthwick, from Greenock and he was seeking Bell's help in setting up a school for several local deaf children. Mr. Bell went to Greenock and started a private school for these children in a room in the Greenock Academy and called it the "Articulation School". As long as the parents could supply the funds for a teacher Bell was able to supply the expertise. At that time Mary True, who had moved from Boston to England and was on vacation from a teaching job, traveled to Greenock, at Bell's invitation, to work as a temporary teacher until a permanent one could be recruited from the United States.

Three weeks later a Mr. Jones arrived and replaced Miss True. By 1883 the local school board became involved and gave the Articulation School a room in the Glebe School. Before long the deaf children were interacting with the "normal" children and receiving lip-reading instruction. Bell sent a Miss Nichols over from the United States to Greenock to train other teachers on the art of lip-reading to the deaf. She also taught the children. The school once again moved to Ardogwan School in 1885 where it had it's own special corner and was called the Nelson Street School. All the changes and moves ended with the school's last name change to Garvel school in late 1885 - a name that it still holds today. By 1968 the school had its very own building. Garvel School (Garvel Deaf Centre as it is now called) still operates today under the guidance of Head Teacher Margaret M Keir. Its' children are integrated into nearly all-mainstream classes.

Bell adored his little deaf children in Greenock and wrote Mabel long letters about them and the new school, ever hopeful that she would share his enthusiasm and come to see them too. She didn't. Something she came to regret later in life.

Top: Mabel & Alec at their Beinn Bhreagh home Baddeck,
Nova Scotia, Canada

Bottom: Mabel, Alexander and their two daughters Elsie & Daisy
(1884/5)

3. D. C. Days

Mabel, Alexander and their daughter, Elsie May, returned to North America in the fall of 1878, landing at Quebec on November 10th. After visiting Bell's parents in Ontario they returned to Cambridge. Mabel was very happy to be back home again in Cambridge. Here she was in her Brattle Street home, one full of many memories, and now she was the mother of the household with a daughter of her own. It felt good. Unfortunately, husband Alec took ill and was in the Massachusetts General Hospital for a while. Mabel's parents, however, were now no longer living in Cambridge and had moved to Washington D.C. Mr. Hubbards' work had taken them there and now Mabel was missing her parents terribly. She was very family orientated and loved having lots of family members around her. It didn't take long for Mabel to persuade Alexander, once he was fully recovered from his illness, to move to D.C. Mabel and her father also persuaded Bell to give up his work as a teacher and to devote himself full-time to the Bell Telephone Company. He agreed and it was a very happy Mabel that moved to D.C. The house in Cambridge was kept and they often returned there during the summer months.

They rented a home on Rhode Island Avenue, only a short walk away from her parents' Twin Oaks home. Mabel had also brought along their housekeeper from England, Mary Home, together with Elsie's nursemaid, Annie. Unfortunately Annie had trouble adjusting to life in the United States and in particular found it difficult working with the black servants. Annie returned to England.

Social life for Mabel in D.C. was very difficult and also very demanding at first. Alexander's work with the Bell Telephone Company kept him away a lot and when he was home he was always busy working on his next invention. Mabel still had trouble getting him to go to bed at a decent hour and this remained a constant sore-point between them throughout their married life. A very devoted wife, she was always there though to give her husband support and helped him constantly with his work, taking down notes, scribbling his thoughts on paper, and even making her own suggestions.

In the fall of 1879 they moved into a new home on 4th Street and on February 15th the following year their second daughter Marian "Daisy" was born. They would always refer to her as Daisy. By now the Bells were financially stable with a yearly income of about $24,000.00 and the Bell Telephone Company had now become the American Bell Telephone Company. Mabel herself owned some 2,975 shares in the company, so it was fair to say that life for the Bells was pretty good.

As time passed by Mabel became happy and content with her new social status in D.C. She began to love living in Washington. Then came the hot summer of 1881. Mabel was pregnant with their third child and decided to take the girls to Pigeon Cove in Massachusetts to escape the heat of Washington. This was also the summer when President James A. Garfield was shot - July 2nd - and the summer when Mabel's husband tried unsuccessfully to help the President. He had been working on a rudimentary metal detector and hoped that it would help locate the bullet lodged in the President's abdomen. He tried twice to locate the bullet but was unsuccessful. One has to wonder if the President had not been lying on a steel coil mattress would Alexander have succeeded and would he have saved the President's life? He did ask for all metal objects to be removed, but the mattress had been overlooked. Mabel, meanwhile, had been keeping track of her husband's failed attempts by reports in the press. She knew that her husband's failure would be very frustrating for him and she shared that frustration. By October of the same year Mr. Bell had perfected his metal detector.

Life is full of bitter ironies and Mabel's was no exception. While Alexander was busy trying to save a life in D.C. their own son, Edward, had been born prematurely on August 15th and lived only a few short hours. His death had resulted from respiratory problems. It was a painful blow to both Mabel and Alexander, and left them both shattered and not in the best of health. In September 1881, they decided to go to Europe to escape their pain and returned the following spring refreshed and healthy.

Once back in D.C. they decided to buy a new and much larger home. This home was on Rhode Island Avenue, like their first rented house had been, only this one took up an entire block at Scott Circle. The three-story pompeiian red brick mansion at number 1500 would be their home for the next seven years. Mabel had extensive renovations done to the home (stables wainscoted in pine, stained glass windows in the oratory and a large conservatory with enameled brick walls) which took over a year to complete and by the time they were finished in the fall of 1883 Mabel found herself pregnant again. On November 17th she gave birth to their fourth child, Robert, who survived only minutes. Mabel had not been well during this pregnancy and here was yet another blow to her and Alexander - the loss of a second son. The next few years brought more than their fair share of sadness to Mabel's family. On October 16th, 1884 Maurice Grossman, husband of her sister Gertrude died and less than a year later Mabel's sister, Berta(Roberta), died from Tuberculosis on July 4th, 1885. Gertrude died a year after that also from Tuberculosis.

As if this hadn't been enough for one family to endure, tragedy struck again in January 1887, when the third floor of their home caught on fire. Everyone escaped without injury and only the third floor was burnt. However, water damage was extensive and it all turned to ice - it was after all January and it was very cold! Mabel, true to form, did not waste anytime and set to work immediately gathering local men to help clean up the mess. One such local man was Charles Thompson. Mabel was greatly impressed by his efforts and hard work and hired him on the spot as a permanent member of her household staff. Mr. Thompson stayed with Mabel and her family for 35 years.

The Rhode Island home was completely refurbished and as good as new but two years later in 1889 the Bells sold it to Levi P. Morton, the then American Vice-President. For the next two years Mabel and family lived in a rented home on 19th Street and finally in 1891 bought what was to be their last D.C. home at 1331 Connecticut Avenue.

1331 Connecticut Ave., N.W. Washington D.C.,
where Mabel & Alec lived from 1892 - 1922

The Study at 1331 Connecticut Ave., N.W. in
Washington, D.C. January 1923

Mabel's dining room at 1331 Connecticut Ave., N. W. Washington D.C. January 1923

During this time Mabel's daughter, Elsie, had been very ill. She suffered from Chorea, a nervous disease that causes uncontrollable spasmodic twitching of the body and is more commonly referred to as St. Vitus' Dance. Mabel had sent Elsie to Philadelphia with a nurse companion where she was cared for by neurologist Dr.S. Weir Mitchell. By the end of 1891 Elsie was feeling much better and was able to return to D.C. to be with her family once again.

Mabel was by now one of the elite of Washington society. She was described as "a charming hostess who receives the stranger with quiet kindliness of manner".[1] She was well known for her Wednesday evening soirees, when a large group of eminent scientists would gather for informal discussions of every known scientific topic. Mabel enjoyed nothing more than having a home full of people. She loved to entertain and oversaw every last detail of preparation for her special evenings.

Amongst the many special and distinguished visitors to the Bell home was Helen Keller. Her father, Arthur H. Keller, brought Helen to see Mr. Bell to ask if he could help Helen who had been blind and deaf since infancy. She was only six on that first visit, but the friendship between Helen and the Bells lasted a lifetime. On a later visit Helen ended up on the stable roof with Mabel's two daughters Elsie and Daisy. "...Mr. Bell, a leading authority on problems of the deaf, consulted with Helen's father, while Elsie and Marian, known to the family as Daisy, took Helen off to play. Half an hour later, the Bells were horrified to find the trio on the roof of the stable. 'Helen had a wonderful time,' Elsie recalled, 'but Daisy and I got the lecture of our lives.'"[2]

1891 was also the year in which The Washington Club officially formed. Mabel together with other society women would meet on a regular basis, once a week at the home of Senator & Mrs. Eugene Hale. There they would sit and discuss many contemporary topics - everything from politics, local and world events, arts and music, to literary developments. At one of their fall meetings they decided to call themselves The Washington Club and so the official club was named. Mabel enjoyed these social gatherings with her fellow socialites and took the idea back with her to Baddeck, Nova Scotia, Canada where she and Bell were then building a new summer home. That fall she founded The Young Ladies Club of Baddeck on October 10th, 1891. (See chapter 7 for more details on this club)

Mabel did not let her deafness affect her social life at all. She acted like a normal hearing person and the only thing that did give away her deafness was her voice. Mabel gave speeches and interacted with all the other women just as if she could hear every word spoken. She even made fun of her deafness and would bang at the dinner table if her daughters were misbehaving and say " If you don't behave I'll close my eyes and won't hear a thing! ".[3] She and husband Alec loved to go to the silent movies and they did go quite often. Mabel especially liked the Western's because they were full of action and she always had a good laugh reading the actors lips - because what they were saying was often not what was being shown on the running scripts at the bottom of the screens! When talking pictures came in all of that changed and Mabel didn't enjoy the movies so much.

Mabel's ability to lip-read was well known. The American Association for the Promotion of Teaching Speech to the Deaf invited her to present a paper on the intricacies and benefits of lip-reading. This paper entitled, " Further Contribution To The Study Of That Subtile Art Which May Inable One With An Observant Eie To Heare What Any Man Speaks By The Moving Of The Lips."[4] was read at their fourth summer meeting at Chautaugua, N.Y., July, 1894. It described in great detail how she came to lip-read, her parents devotion and insistence that she talked, and related many childhood memories (some of them painful) with a sprinkling of humour that kept the reader or listener truly fascinated. She proved herself a very eloquent writer and an extremely remarkable woman. The speech in its entirety can be found at the end of this book.

Life went on as usual in D.C. and in the summer of 1895 Mabel, daughters Elsie and Daisy, and their manservant, Charles Thompson departed for a trip to Europe. They visited Paris, the Channel Islands and Switzerland with husband Alexander joining them sometime in August. They returned to Washington in the fall and both girls were enrolled in boarding school.

December 7th, 1896 was a big day in Mabel's household - it was Elsie's debut to society! Over 500 guests were invited to this grand occasion and were greeted by musicians in the hall as they entered the Connecticut Avenue home. That evening guests enjoyed a very elegant supper followed by dancing. Daughter Elsie was now seeing a lot of a young man by the name of Gilbert Grosvenor, son of Dr. Bell's friend Professor Edwin A. Grosvenor. Love and romance were in the air.

Beinn Bhreagh Hall, Baddeck, Nova Scotia, Canada   ca 1919. Home of Mabel and Alec.

Mabel strolls the grounds at Beinn Bhreagh.

Mabel & family getting ready for a ride – July 1918.

Mabel & Alec on the docks, Cape Breton Island, Nova Scotia ca 1920.

Mabel in 1909

Mabel at Beinn Bhreagh in 1910

Mabel & husband Alec take a walk on the
Beinn Bhreagh Estate, 1920

4. Baddeck Beckons

*H*ad the S.S. Hanoverian not run aground in the summer of 1885 on it's way to Newfoundland, I probably would not have written this book. For it was that misfortune which brought Mabel and her family to Baddeck, Nova Scotia, Canada.

Mabel, Alexander and his father Melville Bell together with their two daughters were on their way to Newfoundland that summer of 1885. Their first stop was in Cape Breton, where they were to take a look at the Caledonia coalmines. Mabel's father had some financial interests in the mines which he owned in partnership with some other Cambridge business men and had asked them to make a stop there on their way to Newfoundland.

As their journey continued they took the paddle steamer, the S.S. Marion across the Bras D'Or lakes and docked at Baddeck overnight. Mabel and her daughters remained aboard the steamer but Alexander decided to go ashore as he wanted to use the telegraph office, which was located at the back of "Telegraph House". He had read of this place in a book written by Charles Dudley Warner called *"Baddeck and that Sort of Thing"* and was curious to see whether it would live up to his expectations. It did! Baddeck was a beautiful place. It was a warm misty evening in early September as Maude Dunlop recalled, telling a friend "he was the most handsomest man she had ever seen."[1] She did not know at the time, who he was and when informed by her mother, Mrs. Dunlop, proprietress of the Telegraph House, that he was the inventor of the telephone, it made no difference. All she was interested in was his looks! Mr. Bell and Mrs. Dunlop struck up an instant friendship. She was from St. John's (where they were headed) and Alexander's father, Melville, had also lived there for some time. They had common interests and conversed easily with one another, taking an instant liking to one another.

The next day Mabel and family continued on their journey, but here fate took hold and the S.S. Hanoverian on which they were now travelling ran aground near the village of Portugal Cove. Everyone was rescued safely and it was decided that they would cancel their trip to St. John's in favour of returning to Baddeck. They stayed several weeks before returning to Washington. Mabel wrote "Baddeck is certainly possessed of a gentle, restful beauty and I think we would be content to stay here many weeks just enjoying the lights and shades on all the hills and isles and lakes."[2] The Bells returned to Baddeck the following summer and from then on they were in Baddeck each and every summer for the rest of their lives. Maude Dunlop fondly remembered her first encounter with Mrs. Mabel Bell during that second visit, "a slender graceful woman in her late twenties, with the gentlest manners, with a sweet sympathetic face framed in the most beautiful soft brown hair"[3] she wrote in a paper that was read at one of the Young Ladies Club of Baddeck meetings. Mabel had certainly made an impression upon the people of Baddeck, just as she was so greatly impressed with the beauty of Baddeck herself. Fate had brought these two together.

As Mabel and family had decided they would be coming to Baddeck each and every summer, they chose to rent a cottage for future visits. The first one they rented was actually a small farmhouse called Crescent Grove. The farmhouse rental also included a cow and Mabel and her daughters had a great time making their own butter! A local businessman, Mr. Arthur McCurdy, had secured the farmhouse for them and he and Mr. Bell soon became close friends. The Dunlop family and Mabel's family were fast becoming old friends too.

The friendship of these two families was also another reason why Mabel loved to return to Baddeck. Mrs. Dunlop's hospitality at The Telegraph House had greatly impressed Mabel. On one occasion Mabel was actually rescued by Mrs. Dunlop's son, Jim, when her boat had drifted far out into the lake. Mabel recalled, "We were strangers and perfectly safe. But he had us on his mind, and presently came after us in his boat and helped us back. I thought at the time it was such a nice thing for him to do and since then I and mine have owed him much pleasure and friendliness."[4]

For her husband, Alexander, Baddeck had another hold on him. It reminded him very much of his beloved Scotland. Mabel and family had fallen in love with Baddeck and its people. Mabel enjoyed riding around Baddeck in her own pony carriage on their summer visits, often bringing with her visitors from the United

States. She took a great interest in the people of Baddeck and was especially impressed with the women's fine handiwork (knitting, weaving, hooked rugs etc.) that adorned many of their homes.

Eventually Mabel and Alexander bought Crescent Grove cottage and enlarged it by adding another floor. Across the bay from this cottage was the Redhead peninsula, which afforded a magnifi cent view of the Bras d'Or Lakes. Mabel and Alexander wanted to own this piece of land and although it took seven years to acquire all twenty acres, they did it without any regrets.

They decided to build themselves a new mansion on this land and by November 1893 Beinn Bhreagh Hall (pronounced Ben VREE-ah) was completed. During the construction of this mansion Mabel and Alexander lived in the "Lodge" which Alexander and his friend and now secretary, Arthur McCurdy, had designed and built in 1889. Beinn Bhreagh is Gaelic for Beautiful Mountain, which it most certainly was and still is today.

As you can well imagine the building of this mansion was no small task. When completed it not only comprised the home itself (a large sprawling wooden construction) but also included a sheep farm, warehouses, 12 miles of roads, stables, a windmill, boathouses, wharves, a dairy, workmen's cottages and large sprawling gardens. The Hall, or "Bell Palace" as it was sometimes called was adorned with treasures and furniture from all over the world that the Bells had accumulated during their many travels abroad. There were ten fireplaces in the mansion and a huge one in the main hall. Beinn Bhreagh Hall also had several towers, sunporches, and verandas. This huge undertaking brought employment for many local people both during and after construction. Mabel always cared about the people in the community and when construction began on their mansion she insisted that cottages be built first for the workers. On the farm, Mabel's husband was experimenting with multi-nippled ewes, which he hoped might bear more than one lamb. This fascinated Mabel, but her big true love was her gardens. She planned and planted her gardens with great care and gained great personal delight from them. Those gardens were a veritable feast for the eyes with an enormous array of flowers. Mabel grew rhododendrons, azaleas, lilies, foxgloves, larkspur, iris, poppies, phlox, asters and lupines - to name just a few! She loved the outdoors and all they had to offer. Eventually she began growing fruits and vegetables and, like her husband, began a little experimenting of her own. On one occasion she wrote to the U.S. Department of Agriculture requesting information on the "use of the dark house for lengthening fruiting season". In her reply thanking them for this information she wrote, " I thought it might be of value in lengthening the ripening of our strawberries".[5] When World War I broke out she started experimenting with drying vegetables in the hopes that it may have been of some benefit to the war effort.

Mabel liked to entertain as much at Beinn Bhreagh as she did in Washington. Daughter, Elsie, recalled one such special occasion when a dinner for some local farmers, invited to discuss Alexander's sheep experiments, turned into a "real banquet" - "My mother was not satisfied just to have an ordinary dinner - she had to arrange for a real banquet with special decorations. She had a long mirror, which she put down, in the center of the table, and she had little trees all around with moss and berries, to represent a lake surrounded by meadows, and then she was at a loss what to do for sheep. The children were staying with her at the time, so she got a lot of candles and melted them, then told the children to make sheep. They set to work and made sheep, which were put around the table. I have some of them still at Beinn Bhreagh, and I prize them very much."[6]

5. *Mabel Takes On New Challenges*

Mabel enjoyed her D.C. life, especially being close to her parents once more since the move from Cambridge. She missed them dearly when she was in Baddeck for the summers. They did often make the trip to Baddeck themselves but not always, as was the case in 1897. Mabel and family had begun to spend more than just summers in Baddeck and so she really treasured the times with her parents. It came as quite a blow to her when on December 11th, 1897 her father died. They had been very close to one another. He had suffered from diabetes late in life and Mabel had been helping her mother take care of him. She was very devoted to her parents.

When Alec returned to Baddeck in the spring of 1898 Mabel remained at Twin Oaks to help her mother take care of her father's papers.

It was whilst going through these papers that Mabel came to the realisation just how much of his life her father had dedicated to the plight of the deaf. Yes she knew he had done much to promote the teaching of the deaf - she herself was living proof of the man's work and determination. However, going through his papers really brought home his life-long work. This was a turning point for Mabel who up until now had been so resistant of her own husband's involvement with the deaf, in fact, of her own deafness, she had never really wanted to associate with deaf people and did not want her daughters to either.

Mabel decided to put together a work, in the form of a book, entitled "The Story Of The Rise Of The Oral Method In America" (as told in the writings of the late Gardiner Greene Hubbard) which after completion she presented to the National Education Association when they next met in Washington. A mature Mabel was now taking great interest in the education of the deaf. She continued to collect and sort both her father's and her husband's papers and letters so that they would be a long-lasting tribute to their life-long work. Today those many letters and writings are kept in Washington at the Volta Bureau (Alexander Graham Bell

Association for the Deaf) and also at the A G Bell Museum in Baddeck, Nova Scotia, Canada, as well as at the Bell Room in the National Geographic Society headquarters in Washington, D.C.

Later that same year, 1898, Mabel and family took a break from everything and embarked on a rather exciting trip to Japan where they were received by the Emperor himself! The girls really enjoyed their trip to Japan and afterwards took to calling their father "Daddysan" - a nickname that stuck for years to come! During that trip Mabel bought herself a lovely Kimono that she wore often when she and Alec spent time alone on their Boathouse (the Mabel of Beinn Bhreagh) at the Bell Estate in Baddeck. She found the Kimono comfortable and easy to wear. Not something too many Victorian ladies would dare to do, but Mabel liked to be comfortable.

With the passing of Mabel's father Alec took over as the new President of the National Geographic Society. His mind however was more involved with his inventions and he began to neglect the magazine, especially in the first year. Mabel and daughters, Daisy and Elsie, soon got him back on track and suggested some improvements to the magazine. Mabel felt the magazine to be too dull and scientific and she and her daughters suggested the addition of more photos to make it more interesting for the readers. This addition to the magazine really turned it around and circulation just went up and up and up. They had successfully turned a "technical" magazine into a "perpetual encyclopedia of current knowledge."[1]

Two years after the trip to Japan, daughter Elsie got engaged to her longtime friend, Gilbert Grosvenor, and the two were married on October 23rd, 1900, at the King's Weigh House Church in London, England. The church was situated one block from Gilbert Street just off Grosvenor Square and of course Elsie herself had been born in England, so there were many special memories to share on that wedding day. The following year, 1901, Mabel was back in London where she was one of many on the streets of London at Queen Victoria's funeral procession. She wrote her daughters of the wonderful seats she had for the occasion and I wonder if she thought about that black silk dress from Paris as Queen Victoria passed by. Sister, Daisy, had meanwhile been studying art in New York with Gutzon Borglum (creator of the "heads" in S. Dakota's Black Hills). She met her husband-to-be at one of the many supper's held at her mother's D.C. home. David Grandison Fairchild came into Daisy's life one evening in November, 1904 - they were married less than a year later in April 1905. For the first year of their marriage they lived in an annex of the Bell family home in D.C., moving later to a home they had built in Maryland.

Elsie's husband, Gilbert, became the editor of the National Geographic in 1903 and was also the Director of the Society and later took over as it's President. This position was passed from son to son and today Mr. Gilbert M. Grosvenor, great-grandson of Mabel, is its president.

Now that Mabel's daughters were both married and leading their own very busy lives she had more time to spend with Alec. She was very much a part of his experimentations - offering advice, suggestions, probing, taking notes and being fully supportive in every sense of the word. It was like it had been in the early days of their marriage. These days Alec spent most of his time at their estate in Baddeck where he had the space and the freedom to create and invent.

Mabel and granddaughter Nancy Bell Fairchild - early 1900's

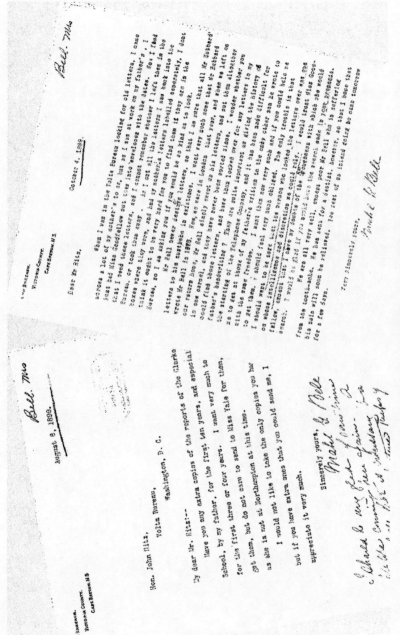

Series of letters Mabel wrote to John D. Hitz requesting copies of letters & reports written by Mr. & Mrs. Hubbard and Mr. Bell.

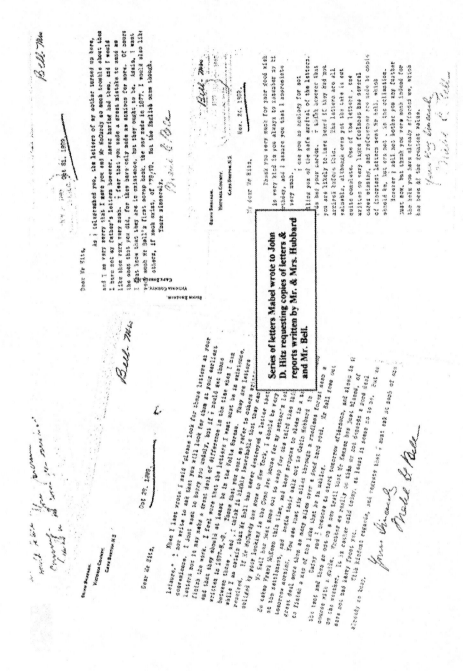

Series of letters Mabel wrote to John D. Hitz requesting copies of letters & reports written by Mr. & Mrs. Hubbard and Mr. Bell.

Alec, Elsie(standing), Daisy and Mabel in chauffeur driven car, ca 1918

Mabel's grandchildren ca 1919

Mabel with her grandchildren on the grounds of Beinn Bhreagh Baddeck, Nova Scotia, Canada 1910

In 1902 Mabel became a grandmother when her first grandchild, Melville Grosvenor, was born to daughter Elsie and husband Gilbert. Mabel had ten grandchildren altogether. Elsie and Gilbert had seven children, Melville, Gertrude, Mabel, Lilian, Carol, Gloria and Alexander, who unfortunately died at the age of five. Daughter Daisy and her husband David Fairchild had three children, Sandy, Nancy and Barbara.

In 1907 Mabel was fully immersed in her husbands work and gave him financial backing to the tune of $20,000.00 to set up the Aerial Experiment Association (AEA). This five-man association officially began on October 1st, 1907 with its objective being for each man to develop a practical flying machine without any restrictions on design. Members Alexander Graham Bell, Glenn H. Curtiss, Lieutenant Thomas E. Selfridge, Casey Baldwin and John A.D. McCurdy did just that and the AEA was dissolved on March 31st, 1909 by terms of the original agreement. The involvement with this association actually made Mabel Hubbard the first woman patron of aviation.

Cars were now a part of everyday life in D.C. and Mabel and husband Alec enjoyed quiet afternoon drives. Mabel's mother bought herself one in 1909. Tragically she died that same year (October) in a car accident. Her chauffeur driven car was rear-ended by a streetcar and they crashed into a pole. Her mother, who was 82 at the time, died instantly. Mabel remained at Twin Oaks that fall in her parents' home and saw to all the details of her mother's estate. Her sister Grace and her husband Charlie Bell moved into her parent's home. The following year Mabel and Alec departed for a trip around the world with friends Frederick and Kathleen Baldwin visiting such places as England, Australia, New Zealand and Hong Kong. Whilst in Hong Kong Mabel took great delight in the harbour there with its population of 40,000 all living in sampans. She would sit up nights on her verandah and just watch the multitude of glistening lights below her in the harbour. It was one of the many experiences she wrote home about. During their time in New Zealand Mabel and Alec visited the one and only school for the deaf in New Zealand. The following year she wrote an article for the Volta Review (a publication of the Alexander Graham Bell Association for the Deaf) describing in full detail her experiences at the Sumner School for the Deaf and the happy and informal place that it was. Mabel enjoyed writing for the Volta Review and over the years made many valuable contributions. Upon their return from their world tour Baldwin and Bell began their work on the hydrofoil hydrodrome boat and Mabel's interests focused on education.

Mabel had read of Dr. Maria Montessori and had become interested in her teaching methods. She decided to visit a Montessori school that had been set up in New York by a Chicago teacher, Miss Anne E. George, and liking what she saw decided to set up a school in D.C. for her own grandchildren. By October of 1912 a Montessori school had been set up in D.C. in an annex of the Bell's home. Enrollment was about 23 and it was now the second Montessori school in North America. She had also established that same year the very first Montessori School in Canada in Baddeck.

She had persuaded an assistant from the New York school, a Miss Roberta Fletcher, to return with her to Baddeck and set up a school there for her grandchildren and also for some of the local children. Mabel's grandchildren and even her own daughters did not really ever think of her as being deaf. To them she was just an ordinary mother and grandmother who set up schools for them, loved them, and was always there for them. They would get her attention by knocking hard on the table or stamping their feet or even waving their hands. They knew they had a grandmother that cared a lot about them and when told not to shout in the house they just naturally assumed it was so as not to disturb Mr. Bell in his study!

When told to talk to grandmother only to her face they just thought that was the polite thing to do and on one occasion daughter Elsie even asked her mother's advice about where to put the orchestra at a dance party for maximum hearing for all the guests! Mabel replied, "Don't you think that is a rather funny question to ask me?"[2] Mabel carried out her life as a normal hearing person and it was so easy to forget she was deaf.

In April of 1913 well over 200 people gathered at Mabel's D.C. home and a committee was formed to establish a permanent Montessori school in Washington D.C. - under the direction of Misses George and Fletcher. Of course a new location had to be found as they could not continue to meet in the Bell home. After some searching Mabel bought a home at 1840 Kalorama Road, which was turned into a school. The Montessori Educational Association was established and Mabel became its first President. Margaret Wilson, daughter of President Woodrow Wilson, was on the Board of Trustees. Their mandate was to establish such schools all across the United States. The system did flourish for a while, especially after Dr. Montessori's visit to the United States in 1914 (she came on a speaking tour) but then it started to die a slow death. By 1919 Mabel had no other choice but to close the school. (For additional information see chapter on Mabel and Education).

In 1913 daughter, Elsie, was an officer in the local branch of the National American Women's Suffrage Association. Mabel was there to help her daughter in the fight for Women's rights - a cause she believed in greatly. A meeting was held at Elsie's home that year and a protest march on Capitol Hill was planned for March 3rd. Mabel and husband Alec cheered the marchers from a grandstand on Pennsylvania Ave. Elsie took four of her six children to take part in the march and they were attacked by angry mobs of men - who even went as far as to pull balloons out of the children's hands and burst them. As an advocate of women's rights, Elsie was becoming very much like her mother Mabel. She too had that sense of community and commitment to making things better for those around her. Elsie was even successful in securing "good jobs" for women at the National Geographic, making it one of the first organizations to do so. When the city of Washington had a problem with bacteria-laden milk in 1916, which posed such a great threat to the children Elsie decided to take action. Local newspapers ignored the problem because they were afraid of losing advertisers but Elsie together with some members of her Twentieth Century Club issued a periodical bulletin listing the milk companies that passed minimum health standards and left out the ones that failed. It wasn't long before the Washington milk supply improved and Congress later passed a strong milk act to enforce purification of the milk supplies. Elsie was truly her mother's daughter.

The same year when Dr. Montessori had visited America in 1914, WWI had broken out in Europe on August 4th. Mabel's husband Alec and his friend Baldwin were busy building boats for the Canadian Navy in Baddeck. They had also hoped to build subchasers for the US Navy but the deal fell through. Mabel ever community minded was doing her part to help the war effort and started to do some experimenting with "drying" vegetables.

In the spring of 1917 the United States entered the war and Mabel, living in D.C. at that time got "caught-up" in the whole excitement of it all. D.C. was "alive" with the war effort. It was at this time that she wrote an appeal for conscription. Her "Women Of America" appeal was printed up by the Naval Department and over 2,500 copies were distributed across the US - all signed by Mabel herself.

Now in her sixties, Mabel was beginning to reflect on her life and children and her grandchildren's futures. She wrote several letters making requests for her final resting place and that of her husband. She also asked her children to take care of their good friends Casey and Kathleen Baldwin and their children.

Alec's health had not been good for quite some time and even when his lifelong friend, Helen Keller, wrote asking that he come to Long Island to be part of the photographic history of her life, Mabel wrote Helen from Baddeck :

July 15th, 1918

"He is dreadfully sorry to refuse any request of yours, and so am I, but I know you will realize how much his life and health mean to me, and that I cannot let him take what I know is a real risk to both."

Affectionately yours,

Mabel G. Bell[3]

Mabel and Alec were now in their last years of life and despite ill-health continued to invent, create and lead productive lives. Mabel enjoyed her writings for the Volta Review and when her dear friend Mary True died in 1921 she set up a foundation in her name to enable a teacher of the deaf to devote some time to an area of study that paid tribute to her lifelong friend. It took the form of a Chair of History and English Literature in the Clarke

School at Northampton, Massachusetts. As Mabel wrote, " She (Miss True) did not care for the more mechanical work of teaching the formation of vocal utterance, what she loved was to help in the unfolding of the dormant minds, to see the dull eyes brighten as new ideas were comprehended. Most of all, as you of course knew, you - who she so much loved and admired, - she enjoyed telling them the stories of old, of great men and great deeds of the past. So by logical sequence, it seems to me we come to some kind of foundation whereby her name is connected with History and Literature."[4]

The winter of 1921/22 was fast approaching and Mabel and Alec decided to take a trip to the Caribbean for some sun and relaxation. It was their last vacation together and one that they thoroughly enjoyed.

Alec died on August 2nd, 1922. It came quickly. Mabel was sat with him on the porch of their Beinn Bhreagh home holding his hand in the moonlight to the very end. As US and British flags hung at half-mast, the funeral procession sang, "Bringing in the Sheaves". Alec was buried on the grounds of the Beinn Bhreagh Estate in a simple pine coffin lined with Aeroplane linen. His grandchildren made a pall of green balsam fir and the only flowers were on the wreath from the Telephone Company. Laurel for victory, sheaves of wheat for gathered harvest and pink roses for his gentleness and sweetness.

The gravesite had been blasted out of the rock on the Beinn Bhreagh Estate and lined with fir boughs. The coffin was placed in a steel vault, just in case he might be moved later to the USA. He wasn't. Even though her loss was so great Mabel continued to carry on with her husbands work overseeing all his projects. She gave a ten-year contract to Baldwin (at $10.000.00 a year) to carry on with his experiments; she took care of the sheep and became a member of the Board of Trustees (replacing her husband) for the Clarke School for the Deaf.

She didn't really want to go back to her D.C. home but did return around December of 1922. Her health was now too on the decline. Doctors discovered she had cancer. She went to stay with her daughter Daisy in Maryland and died there on January 3rd, 1923 around 8 pm. Some say she died of a broken heart, but whether it was that or the cancer her death was a great blow to all whom had known her. Just one hour before her death Mabel had received a telegram informing her that she had been given honorary membership in the Telephone Pioneers of America. She was indeed a great pioneer. Her funeral took place at her parents Twin Oaks home in Washington, D.C. at 3 pm on Friday January 5th. It was a very simple service conducted by Rev. Dr. Charles Wood of the Church of the Covenant. A simple service as requested by Mabel herself. She was then cremated.

Her ashes were placed in her husbands' grave on August 7th at a brief service that took place at 5pm - exactly one year later after her husband's funeral. Why 5pm? That had been the time she had always joined Alec at his laboratory each and every day to drive him back home.

Many tributes were made to Mabel after her death. She had been the kind of person that made a long-lasting impression on anyone that came into contact with her. Many were moved and touched by this remarkable woman.

"Graceful writer, charming hostess, noble wife. In any Hall of Fame of America's great women she will stand, by right!"[5]

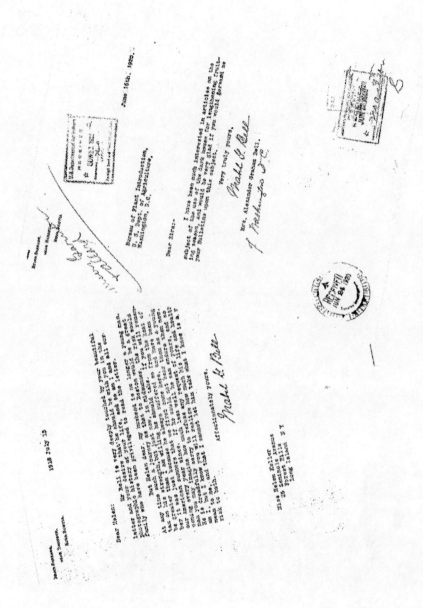

Helen Keller enjoyed a very special friendship with both Mabel & Alec.

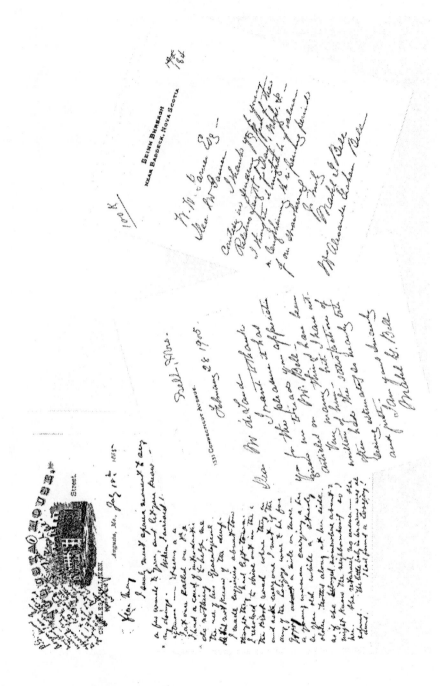

BEINN BHREAGH
NEAR BADDECK, NOVA SCOTIA

1921 October 4.

My dear Mrs Lyman,

This is to ask your help and co-operation in the establishment of a Memorial to Miss True.

It is proposed to take the form of a Chair of History and English literature in the Clarke School at Northampton.

The appropriateness of establishing a memorial to Miss True at Clarke lies in the consideration that Clarke is in a very direct way the result of Miss True's work. While Mr Clarke made the building of the School possible through his money, and others helped, my father, Mr Hubbard was the originator of the plan to start a school for the deaf on the oral method, and it was his energy and initiative that brought the thing to pass.

He could not have had the certainty that the idea of teaching little deaf children to speak and read the lips, if his own little daughter had not proved it to his satisfaction, and more than all it could not have carried conviction to the others whose co-operation was necessary to success, had not her attainments convinced these. That they did was Miss True's triumph. Clarke School was the sequel.

This fact has never I think been adequately recognized, and it is therefor all the more fitting that those who knew Miss True, and appreciated what a great teacher she was, how wonderful and brilliant her accomplishment was, under the circumstances, the disadvantages against which she had to struggle, including not only her own inexperience, but the entire lack of precedent for every step she took in the instruction of her pupil, should emphasize her claim to consideration by the placing of her memorial in this, the first successful, permanent Oral School in America.

In almost Miss True's last letter to me written a few days before she died she could she wished it were not wrong to hope that she might be allowed to teach little deaf children in the world whether she was going, for that was her ideal of Heavenly bliss. It seems to me therefor that you would agree that it would be in accordance with her wishes, and in every way a wonderful thing, if we could make it possible to associate her memory with the kind of work she loved, in the school that so largely owes it's inception to her genius for teaching.

She did not care especially for the more mechanical work of teaching the formation of vocal utterance, what she loved was to help in the

unfolding of the dormant minds, to see the dull eyes brighten as new ideas were comprehended. Most of all, as you of course know, you-who she so much loved and admired,-- she enjoyed telling them the stories of old, of great men and great deeds of the past.

So by logical sequence, it seems to me we come to some kind of foundation whereby her name is connected with History and literature.

Her sister, Mrs Gehring is most sympathetic to the plan, and agrees that it is the most appropriate place and memorial, and has offered to contribute a thousand dollars if a sufficient sum can be raised to insure the fit carrying out of the idea. I of course will also contribute. I have no idea how much money would be needed, but think it should be sufficient to yield an income that would enable half at least of one teacher's time being devoted to that special branch of study, -- say five hundred a year. I would in fact like to aim for ten thousand.

What do you say, and what do you suggest that we could do? I asked Mrs Gehring for the names of those of Miss True's friends whom she had met through Dr Gehring, but she replied that she felt that she had already drawn on them as much as she could in re-establishing a Bethel Academy where their father had taught, and Miss True had been educated.

That of course would commend itself to those who had known Miss True simply as a sweet and brilliant woman of intellect, but is quite inadequate to commemorate the great work she accomplished, in demonstrating for the first time before the public, that deaf children could not only be taught to speak and understand speech, but educated beyond the average of school children.

Now I now wish I, the child in question, had been more worthy of very certain knowledge that I could have done better if I had not been so incorrigibly lazy. I dont envy Helen Keller her talents, but I do envy her her strong will and great ambition to excel. If Miss True and my mother but had had such a character to work with their fame would have gone around the world. That is the utterly discouraging thing about being a teacher. The most can chose his marble or bronze, the teacher must often put her best work on inferior children. --

I see that my excitement is interfering with the accuracy of my typewriting, so I best shut up !

Much love to you and yours,

Affectionately
Mabel G Bell

Letters of Mabel and Alexander Graham Bell

happiness in the future. The Hospital continues to do good work under the supervision of Miss Hodds, and there is every prospect that 1910 will be as successful as the previous years have been.

A. ROSAMOND, Secy.-Treasurer.

P. C. McGREGOR, President.

HARBOUR, N.S., MARCH 1ST, 1910.

To MISS McRASLIE,
SUPT. VICTORIAN ORDER OF NURSES,
OTTAWA.

Greetings from your modest little District by the Sea.

Another year has glided into the shadows since my last report and with the Christ we leave the pages of that effort to kindness the Guild. As we look back upon these months we feel that the Order has brought untold benefits to the afflicted, year by year we notice a fast appreciation of this aim of the Order among the people. Now it is patent to all that to care in a proper way for the sick a trained nurse is essential. This being established the prejudices of the past belong to the past.

Fortunately no epidemic had to be handled in this district during the year, and although our course was not much of the time idle, yet she was not called upon to do the hardest work of the preceding year. All in all last year has had a smooth, easy year, with no complaints from the sick or the people.

We are not overburdened with the goods of this world in this remote corner, but the committee manage to keep accounts evened up in a way that makes some of us wonder how it is done.

Mrs. Alexander Graham Bell continues her charitable interest in the Order, by her annual subscription of $100.00.

Your Committee tried many methods to raise funds—Charity balls did not take, as we are not given to dancing; the "Bean Supper" might do in Massachusetts, but not here; Moonlight excursions were tried with some effect at first until all our young people were married off. A happy inspiration to the chief lady members of the Committee come to the reverend gentleman of our town, and the result is a series of monthly lectures, which are proving a brilliant success from a literary and financial viewpoint.

By dancing we have appealed to the love of our neighbours, by the books to their intellectual concerns to their health; but we have found this appeal to their love by lectures—a mental diet and one that has touched the popular fancy better than all others.

The ever-patient and faithful Miss Crocker left us in September, and I am pleased to say her successor bids fair to be as efficient and popular.

I have here to thank the Committee one and all for their promptness and faithfulness in attending meetings and planning and carrying out methods of entertainments to raise funds. I also have to thank the reverend gentlemen of this town with their good people who have so generously aided us in keeping up the Victorian Order in this district.

Respectfully submitted,

DANIEL McDONALD, Chairman.

34

MRS. A. G. BELL DIES AT HOME OF DAUGHTER

Widow of Telephone Inventor, Failing Since His Death, Succumbs at 64.

By Universal Service.

WASHINGTON, Jan. 4.— Mrs. Alexander Graham Bell, widow of the inventor of the telephone, is dead at the home of her daughter Mrs. David Fairchild, Chevy Chas Md. She was sixty-four.

Her health had been failing si the death of her husband last F ner, from the shock of which had never recovered, it was s members of the family. F arrangements have not beer but it is probable that she I buried beside the body of in Nova Scotia.

Surviving, besides Mrs are another daughter, N Grosvenor, wife of the the National Geograj and a sister, Mrs. Cr wife of a prominen banker.

FATHER AIDED

Remarkable hers ways and holding the scientific wor given full credit has success in phone. He oft inspiration w continue his she literally Philadelphia Exposition phone was She was ter of Gard Cambridge Dr. Bell' first prev vived her Compan and De romat large taught vantor. however, after she had reached the ag three.

Mrs. Alexander G. Bell.

It would be only fitting that the name of Mrs. Alexander Graham Bell, the widow of the inventor, who has just died, should appear with his on any monument erected in his honor, for it is said that it was because of her that he was led to make the experiments that were to result in the development of the telephone as a necessity of life and business.

Mrs. Bell as a result of an attack of scarlet fever was stone deaf from early childhood. In an effort to help her to hear, her husband turned to the great business of his life.

It was also through the efforts of Mrs. Bell's father, Gardner Greene Hubbard, that reading the lips in stead of the sign language has been utilized in the education of the deaf. The case of Mrs. Bell, who survived her husband only five months, is a striking instance of the way in which the affliction of the individual may be turned to the benefit of the many.

Bell... She became... had reached...

... Lip Reading ... advantage... overcome her if me to be widely cultured deaf we She mastered the and learned to a a number of lan ... ied in France an

... ean particularly no ... rest in education By perfecting a ... reading, she virtually ... the sign language amo She wrote a book method of teaching if to speak. She was a freque tributor to magazines on tional topics.

In the National Capital Mrs. was best known for the Wednesday evening soirees at her Connecticut avenue home. Every Wednesday evening she was in the city a large group of eminent scientists would gather for informal discussions of every known scientific topic.

...he Rev. Dr. Charles Wood, a Church of the Covenant, will duct a simple service at Mrs. ...s request. The body will be ...ated and later the ashes will buried beside the body of Dr. ...ander Graham Bell, at Bein ...agh, near Baddeck, Nova Scotia. ...rs. Bell died at the home of her ...ghter, Mrs. David Fairchild, in ...ry Chase, Md. shortly after ... ...lock last night.

...th of her famous ...band ... Bell's health

HELPED DEAF PERSON

...es th ...ed th ability to overcome her bee Mrs. Bell came to be the wide over as the means of the most cultured deaf ...t in the world. She mastered the ...rs of lip-reading and learned ...verses fluently in a number ...nguages. She studied in Fran Germany.

She was particularly noted her interest in education of children. By perfecting a mea of upreading, she virtually bro down the sign language among d people. She wrote a book on th oral method of teaching the dea to speak, and also was a frequen contributor to magazines on educa tional topics.

In the national capital Mrs. Bell was best known for the Wednesday soirees at her Connecticut avenue home. Every Wednesday evening she was in the city a large group of eminent scientists would gather for informal discussions of every scien tific topic.

Mrs. Alexander Graham Bell, widow of the inventor of the telephone whose death last night was hastened by grief over the recent loss of her famous husband.

MRS. ALEXANDER GRAHAM BELL.

FUNERAL RITES FOR MRS. BELL PLANNED

Widow Never Recovered From Shock of Husband's Death in Nova Scotia.

The funeral of Mrs. Alexander Graham Bell, widow of Alexander Graham Bell, inventor of the telephone, will take place Friday afternoon at 3 o'clock at Twin Oaks, home of Mrs. Charles J. Bell, her sister.

Twin Oaks formerly was the home of Mrs. Bell's father, Gardiner Greene Hubbard, organizer and first president of the Bell Telephone Company.

...aphic Society, w ...ty of Grace Hubbard had a ...of Charles J. Bell, grand son of ...American Security and Trust ...ompany. She is also ...e grandchildren, and survived by ...Had received a telegram from ...a J. Curry notifying her from ...had been electing her that ...bership in the Telephone Pic ...s of America. ...oceherself in many other ...scientific would Mrs. Bell was ...nd holding a high place in the ... full credit by her husband ...s success in perfecting the ... He often said ...inspiration that caused him ... literally made him so to ...s experiments that ...pen for the Centennial Ex ...in 1876, was the telephone ...onstructed.

...s Mabel Hubbard, daughter ...iner Greene Hubbard, ...ass., then ...ted Dr. Bell's experiments ...the first president of the ...phone Company, ...s after the Centennial she ...hen were married. Their ...hen as one of ...of deaf children so ...to talk by the telephone

Wash. Times
Jan. 4, 1923

Mabel & Alec on the docks at Beinn Bhreagh (1920)

Mabel loved her flower gardens at Beinn Bhreagh (1919)

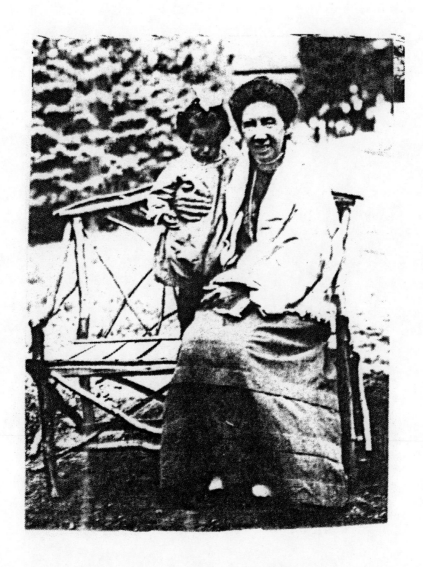

Mabel & granddaughter Lilian Grosvenor 1908

Part II

Mabel's Legacy

6. Contributions To The Baddeck

Community

*I*n 1894 Mabel set up the Home Industries of Baddeck. From the time of her first visit to Baddeck Mabel had been very impressed with the handiworks of the local women, which were displayed in their homes. She decided to bring in needlework teachers from Montreal and the United States to "fine-tune" their work and thus started a thriving cottage industry for the women of Baddeck. One of the first displays of the women's fine work was at The Telegraph House and for some of the women it was their first income earned too - a first step towards financial independence gained through the production of quality produce.

Mabel was also busy on the social front for the women of Baddeck. Three years earlier she had established The Young Ladies Club of Baddeck on October 10th, 1891. She enjoyed her social gatherings in Washington with other women and was a member of The Washington Club. She decided that the women of Baddeck would benefit from such a club and so it was formed. Women gathered together to discuss local and world events, travel, books and art. The purpose of the club as stated in their constitution was "to stimulate the acquisition of general knowledge and to promote sociability among the young of Baddeck."[1] No greater was the need than for those women in remote Baddeck. Once again Mabel showed the depth and warmth that she felt for the people of Baddeck. This club still survives today and is probably the oldest women's club in all of Canada. Today the club is known as The Alexander Graham Bell Club in honor of Mabel's husband. Chapter seven of this book explains the club in more detail.

When there was a need for a new library in Baddeck Mabel came to the rescue (she had been a great lover of books from an early age). She bought a disused church and had it renovated to become the very first public library of Baddeck. It bears the name Gertrude Hall and was just another example of Mabel's concern for the community in which she lived.

In 1895 she established the first Canadian Home and School

Association in Baddeck when she encouraged parents interested in the education and welfare of their children to form such a group. Mrs. Bell had been in contact with similar groups of parents in Washington who at that time were planning the First National Congress of Mothers for 1897. She saw the need for the people of Baddeck and motivated them to organize an official association. That very first meeting was held on the 18th of December 1895 in the Academy Building, Baddeck. Soon after that first meeting parents and teachers across the country began to meet and form their own associations at the local level. These associations are still going strong today more than 100 years later. The Canadian Home & School, Parent-Teacher Federation (which recently changed its name to the Canadian Home & School Federation - CHSF) is a federation of provincial and local parent-teacher groups which promotes the welfare of children and youth, raises the standards of home life, fosters cooperation between parents and teachers, fosters high ideals of citizenship, and, through education promotes international peace and goodwill. Ideals and standards that I am sure Mrs. Bell would approve of.

Mabel was also concerned about the health and well being of the people in the community and she often wondered what would happen if someone became ill and was in need of a doctor. It was a rural area and accidents were bound to happen on the farms. She wondered what could be done so that the people could prepare themselves and assist until a doctor could be reached. So Mabel brought in a doctor, Dr. Kerr, to give a lecture and teach basic first aid to the women. Dr. Kerr gave an "Emergency Class" to the women and provided them with notebooks to keep a written account of some basic emergency care techniques. Yet another way in which Mabel showed her concern for the community of Baddeck.

In the late 1800's Mabel struck up a friendship with Lady Aberdeen, the then wife of the Governor General of Canada. She visited Beinn Bhreagh Hall on many occasions.

Mabel saw the need for better health care in Baddeck and together with Lady Aberdeen managed to bring the very first Victorian Order of Nurses (V.O.N.) to Baddeck. At that time even the people of Sydney did not have such services. The Baddeck branch of the V.O.N. opened in 1898. One year earlier, in 1897, Canadian Prime Minister, Sir Wilfred Laurier, had officially approved the order as a memorial for Queen Victoria's Diamond

Jubilee. Reports were sent on a regular basis back to Ottawa to the Superintendent of the V.O.N. and on one such occasion the local Baddeck Chairman, Daniel McDonald, wrote, "Mrs. Alexander Graham Bell continues her charitable interest in the Order by her annual subscription of $100.00".[2] In that same letter of March 1st, 1910, to Superintendent McKenzie he wrote, "Greetings from your modest little District by the sea. Another year has glided into the shadows since my last report and with it have passed our little efforts to follow the Golden Rule. As we look back upon those months we feel that the Order has brought untold benefits to the afflicted, year by year we notice a just appreciation of the aim of the Order among the people."[3] His letter further related to the ups and downs of fundraising for the Order noting that balls and bean suppers were not for the people of Baddeck. However, they did seem to prefer a series of monthly lectures, which appealed to their "mental diet" rather than their feet or stomachs! Just a year after that letter was written with so much optimism, it is sad to note that the Order was closed in 1911 due to lack of funds. There is only so much fundraising that can be done in such a small community.

In the summer of 1912 Mabel set up The Children's Laboratory at the Beinn Bhreagh Estate. This was the very first Montessori school in Canada. Mabel had read much about Dr. Maria Montessori and was greatly impressed by her "new method" of teaching. She had visited a Montessori school in New York and decided to set one up for her grandchildren. She persuaded Miss Roberta Fletcher, assistant at the New York school, to travel to Baddeck and assist in the setting up of the school. It was attended by Mabel's grandchildren together with their friends and children from the community from the age of three and upward. She felt the children of the community would also benefit from this new style of education. Later that same year in the fall of 1912 she set up another Montessori school in Washington for her grandchildren who lived there. Other local children also attended that Washington school and the attention it attained led to the formation of the Montessori Educational Association of America. Mabel became the first President of the Association.

Although Mabel and her family spent mostly summers in Baddeck, they did on occasion stay there during the winter months. Mabel loved the snow and enjoyed riding in the huge sleigh. One Christmas she invited all the local children over to the Lodge - about thirty in total - for some Christmas celebrating. She had gifts for all of them sent in from Montreal and they were all given candies and an apple before they left. What a treat it must have been for those children. She also enjoyed writing and putting on plays for the community.

As head of the household at Beinn Bhreagh Mabel kept track of all the accounts and was also responsible for paying the salaries. She collected the reports from the various estate department heads and was also in charge of the gardens. Those gardens were her pride and joy with seeds brought back from far and wide during her many travels abroad. She created her own "world of flowers" at Beinn Bhreagh. "She adored the custom of flower-viewing in Japan and so on one occasion invited 100 restless, energetic young lads from the local Academy to a trip to far-off lands - seen through the language of her transplanted flowers. And she was mother enough to know that more than minds must be nourished and so fed the lads (in four relays) and sent each home with a story-book bouquet."[4] So typical of her care and concern for others, always wishing to enhance the knowledge of others.

Beinn Bhreagh Hall was never a quiet place when the Bells were at home. Mabel loved to entertain and was constantly organizing teas, suppers and luncheons. Some were for royalty, some for family and friends, and some for the local people. No matter who the guest, though, Mabel always treated each occasion with great enthusiasm and pride. All guests were treated equal! Once a year she would put together a great Harvest Home Celebration for the men and women who worked on the estate. They together with their families would spend the entire day at Beinn Bhreagh celebrating, eating, dancing and socializing. The big barn was set up with tables and chairs and food was laid out for all. There were sandwiches of all descriptions, cakes, pies, tea, coffee and several barrels of gingerale for all to enjoy. The barn was decorated with vegetables and flowers and upstairs in the loft an area was cleared for dancing. A fiddler played for everyone's' enjoyment and games were organized outdoors for both children and adults.

Prizes were awarded for stiltwalking, hammer tossing, shot put, the potato race and running. I'm sure the people of Baddeck looked forward to this event every year and it was yet another example of Mabel's generosity and caring for her community. Later on in 1915 she even organized a Garden Fete for the benefit of the Red Cross with games and exhibits, refreshments and even homegrown produce for sale.

It came as no surprise then that the people of Baddeck showed their respect and admiration for this wonderful and remarkable woman by passing an ordinance giving her the right to a Canadian vote.

During World War I the Bells were living year-round at Beinn Bhreagh and the workers there were involved with building ships for the Navy. Women as well as men undertook this challenge, becoming perhaps the first female boat-builders in Canadian history. Mabel at this time also set up a miniature, canning factory to preserve the farm's abundant fruits and vegetables. She sought out new and varied ways to cook the limited foods available during those troubled times and by 1917 had become fascinated with the study of nutrition. When the great explosion of the munitions ship happened in Halifax harbour on the morning of December 6th, 1917, Mabel did not hesitate for a minute and had sewing machines transforming old fabrics into children's clothing immediately. The blast was felt at Beinn Bhreagh (some 177 miles from Halifax) as windows rattled and Mabel ever thoughtful and concerned for others well-being wasted no time in sending off packages of clothing and blankets to the survivors in Halifax.

The war effort was in full swing at Beinn Bhreagh and Mabel had everything under control. When 14 of the naval boats had been completed Mabel organized a celebration for the forty or more workers. Once again she had her large mirror laid across the huge dining room table and this time it was bedecked with moss, trees of all descriptions, and finally fourteen silver paper models of boats ! Mabel loved detail. She toasted the "unsung soldiers of Canada", but as everyone laughed and raised their glasses, husband Alexander silently mouthed another toast "To the Lady of Beinn Bhreagh."[5] A truly remarkable lady indeed who gave so much to the people and the community of Baddeck.

Alec, Elsie & Mabel spend time at the beach, Nova Scotia, 1919

Mabel, Alec, family & friends out for a walk on the docks. ca 1919

Mabel Hubbard Girls Help Fight Polio

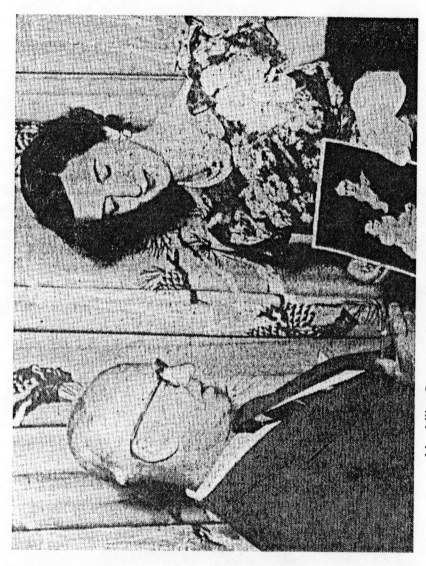

Mrs. Lilian Grosvenor Jones, granddaughter of Mabel Hubbard is the guest of honour at the Clubs' 25th Anniversary in 1958 Montreal, Canada

Mabel Hubbard Club's Annual Spring Fashion Show April, 1939

Students from the Montreal Oral School for the Deaf try out new hearing aids
purchased by the Mabel Hubbard Club, April 1964.

Page 1 of a circular distributed to women's clubs seeking their support for the movement.
Reprinted from " Through The Years " published by National Congress of Parents and Teachers

7. *Young Ladies Club Of Baddeck*

(The Alexander Graham Bell Club)

*I*nspiration for this club came from the Washington Club of which Mabel was a member and it is probably the longest running women's club in Canada today - perhaps the oldest in North America or even the world! Originally called the Young Ladies Club of Baddeck its name was changed in 1922 to the Alexander Graham Bell Club in honour of Mabel's husband, a title that it still holds today.

After her experiences with the Washington Club Mabel decided this would be a wonderful opportunity for the women of Baddeck. A chance to get together and "learn", socialize, etc. These women in Baddeck were far removed from society at large and were in great need of such intellectual stimulation. She organized the first meeting, which was held at the Lodge, Mabel's Baddeck home while Beinn Bhreagh Estate was being built, on October 10th, 1891.

When that first meeting took place on October 10th, 1891 Mabel sent over a large rowboat to Baddeck to bring back to the Lodge the women who were interested in forming this new club. In a room filled with autumn leaves, a huge log fire burned in the hearth while women sat around and listened to the by-laws and constitution of this new club. The women further discussed their plans for future meetings and programs. One of the challenges they faced however was lack of resources. If the women were to talk about current affairs etc., they needed the information to properly prepare themselves for their readings. Never one to let anything hold her back, Mabel soon solved this problem by subscribing to several magazines and newspapers for all the members to share. At this time there was no public library in Baddeck - another problem that Mabel took care of at a later date! Apparently the only problem with the subscriptions was that members were not passing along the various magazines and papers to other members when they were supposed to!

In lieu of maps to illustrate travels and geographical talks the women made their own on the backs of wrapping papers and hung them up on the curtains. All members participated in the meetings. Some would read papers, some would sing and all were encouraged to discuss the topics afterwards. In the early meetings they discussed Dickens, Cairo, Kipling, Common Sense In Surgery, How Sponges Live - the topics were varied and it seems like nothing was left out. Since the acquisition of knowledge on a wide variety of subjects was one of the main objectives of the club, such discussions were quite in order.

The "News of the Week" (local news and gossip) was a regular feature of the club meetings and travel was one of the hot topics too. The Bells traveled extensively throughout their lifetime and the women of Baddeck loved to hear about these fascinating tales of travel. Mabel would often read "travel" stories and husband Alexander would give lantern slide shows too. Even when the Bells were travelling abroad, Mabel would send long letters to the club describing her impressions of the countries they visited. These fascinating and illuminating letters would often be read aloud at meetings for all to enjoy.

Over time the meetings began to take on "themes" such as "The Scottish Evening", and one year was devoted entirely to science and another to famous authors.

Although this was a "women's'" club, men were not excluded from the meetings and did attend on several occasions giving talks on all matter of subjects. A doctor once explained how he had removed a needle from a man's foot with the help of Mr. Bell's X-Ray machine and Mr. Baldwin attended once to speak about the "radio".

Ghost stories, fortune telling, housecleaning, poetry, Women's Suffrage, and royalty were all covered in the clubs meetings. It was a certainty that these women were gaining a vast array of knowledge from these meetings. They were also gaining a sense of sociability. Despite Mabel's deafness she never let it get in the way of her social life and was quite the "talker" both here in Baddeck as well as in Washington at the Washington Club.

Today this club still meets every second Thursday from October to April, taking turns at each other's homes. Birthdays, weddings and the like were always celebrated and still are at meetings. The Board of Governors meets during the summer and they make all the plans for the coming year. Subjects, speakers and hostesses are well prepared far in advance. On a rare occasion extra meetings may be held to accommodate a special visitor or speaker. A program is printed up for the year and given to all members at the first meeting in October.

What keeps this group going so strong for so many years? Perhaps because nobody is asked to raise funds for every cause going? More likely though its the enthusiasm of these women (and men) who enjoy the challenge of "acquiring knowledge". There never seemed to be any bickering or rivalry at these meetings. It was and still is simply people getting together to socialize and enhance their gray matter.

Lilias M. Toward, Q.C., remembered well her first meeting. "The first meeting I attended was held at Beinn Bhreagh. Framed in the doorway I saw perhaps fifty people sitting around a large fireplace. I know they were the same people I met daily in the village street, but here was an elegance of dress and a beauty of colour. What was even more surprising was the presence of a number of men, for then I did not know that since the inception of the club its occasional open meetings are looked forward to by the men in the community. So remote from the daily life of our little village did this social gathering appear that it seemed as if I were in a different world where anything might happen. I would not have been surprised to have caught a glimpse of the distinguished figure of Dr. Bell leading his wife down the wide oak staircase to join their friends and neighbours of Baddeck as they had done so often in the past."[1]

Times have changed but the club hasn't - it still thrives today promoting that thirst for knowledge and sociability. Subject matters have changed but the purpose of the club remains intact. A long lasting tribute to its founder Mabel Hubbard.

8. *The Mabel Hubbard Club*

*T*he invention of the telephone not only brought with it great opportunities for world communication but also created many job opportunities for women. Once the telephone became a public service, telephone exchanges were popping up in every city. For women this brought "new employment opportunities" as most if not all of these jobs were filled by women. Back in 1880 women could earn as much as $12.00 a month as an operator!

It didn't take long for these women to start organizing themselves and in 1894 the Lady Operators Benefit Association was formed in Montreal. The women paid an initial 50 cents membership fee and then paid a monthly fee of 15, 20 or 30 cents according to their means. Then if the women became sick they were able to collect a weekly benefit of $2, $3 or $4, depending on how much they had paid into the fund. These women were taking care of themselves.

By 1929 the number of female employees at Bell Canada in Montreal was quite large. Miss Doris Penfold, secretary to Mr. Haskell, who was the then assistant to the vice-president in charge of personnel, recognized a greater need for these young women. She suggested organizing a club for them. A club where the women could get together after-hours, meet, socialize and perhaps work together for the benefit of others. Mr. Haskell was in agreement with Miss Penfold and so she set about talking to the women in the various departments of the company. They would chat during lunch and talk about the benefits of such a club. The idea began to catch on and the women were definitely interested in getting this club off the ground. Miss Penfold started to lay down the foundation for the club. She sought out girls with tact, sociability and compassion who would form the "executive" of the club and put together a provisionary constitution and program outline. These women - about twelve in total - met in Mr. Haskell's office on February 24th, 1933 to discuss their plans for the club. The women represented several departments of the Bell

Telephone Company at the Beaver Hall Building in Montreal. They came from the traffic, commercial, plant, and revenue and disbursements accounting departments. Women were no longer just operators at Bell. They held many and varied positions in the company.

By February 28th, 1933 an announcement appeared in the Beaver Hall Club Bulletin announcing the founding of the club, "Nothing new under the sun? Possibly not, but we think the following idea is pretty new - and good. It concerns every Bell woman employee in Montreal. Ready? Not long ago an idea got itself adopted by an enthusiastic group, and after a session of discussion and debate and some surgical amputation and rejuvenation emerged to find itself an upstanding little fellow answering to the name of "club". "Club", of course, is just in its babyhood. It hasn't even been christened. But it's immensely keen on growing up into a big strong organization, because, like all young things, it's shockful of confidence. And so is the little group, which gave it its start in life. But "club" can only go on living if it receives the interested support of all Bell women… Everyone may belong. We sincerely hope everyone will. There will be an annual fee of twenty-five cents." [1] Mr. J. R. Fletcher, President of the Beaver Hall Club finished off his bulletin by saying , "I commend to you this new group which is affiliated with the Beaver Hall Club. I hope all our representatives will give this group the support accorded all other activities."[2] I wonder if he knew then the tremendous impact this group of women would have on their community and the great service they would afford their fellow employees both male and female?

The first general meeting of the club was held on March 14th, 1933 in Montreal. Members of the club were introduced and a provisionary constitution read. Committees were also appointed to deal with programming, publicity, welfare and membership. The aims of the club were to foster esprit de corps among the women employees, afford a common meeting place for them, offer educational advantages to members via speakers and lectures, give aid to those in need, and mean something definitely worthwhile to each and every member - aims and goals both worthy and meaningful.

Miss Ruth Young (nee Baillie) was the first President, with

club founder, Doris Penfold, serving as the chairman of the Program Committee. The club still lacked a name, however, and it was the subject of much debate. It was decided that the name, when chosen, must have some bearing on the telephone industry. Mr. J. M. Hay, a sales and development manager, suggested the name Mabel Hubbard, wife of telephone inventor, Alexander Graham Bell! No better name could have been chosen and it was unanimously accepted. Miss Penfold wrote to Mabel's daughter, Elsie Grosvenor, asking permission to use the name. Mrs. Grosvenor gave permission and the club became officially known as The Mabel Hubbard Club of the Bell Telephone Company of Canada.

During their first year of operation, The Mabel Hubbard Club organized fashion shows, bridge parties, talent nights, a handicraft exhibit (which lasted two days) and many lectures.

Attendance was very good at all events with an average attendance of 221 people. During their two-day craft exhibit about 850 visitors looked over the 350 different exhibits displayed. As Ruth Young noted, "We were just a bunch of teenagers but we were enthusiastic and ready to try anything. We were young and it just seemed the natural thing to do."[3] Welfare work also played an important role in the clubs activities. Christmas baskets were made up for needy families and on a regular basis some families received coal, milk, clothing and groceries.

It must be noted here that Bell Canada employees were no strangers to community work. It was not unusual for Bell trucks to be seen on the streets of Canadian cities delivering Christmas baskets to those in need. In 1915 telephone operators were sewing and making bandages for servicemen and contributing a day's salary to the Patriotic Fund. They were helping with the war effort and also taking care of the families at home.

By July of 1934 membership in the Mabel Hubbard Club totaled 564, increasing to 869 by July of 1937, and in October 1940, 1004 women were members of the club. From 1940 until the end of 1945 the club suspended its operations due to World War II. A Red Cross Branch of the Mabel Hubbard Club was set up during that time.

On the evening of April 22nd, 1946 the first post-war executive was elected. Around 125 Montreal district members met for tea at the Beaver Hall Building cafeteria in a setting Mabel Hubbard would have loved. Tables adorned with candles and displays of snapdragons, daffodils, carnations and sweetpeas set the mood for their five o'clock tea! Mabel's love for flowers and table decor was well known. And so by the spring of 1946 the club was back in the swing of things and by May of 1947 membership stood at 1700!

The 1949-50 executive had as its goal to bring every single female employee at Bell, Montreal, into their fold. It didn't quite reach that goal but the good work of the club continued on. In 1949 club members helped with the "Fight Polio" campaign in Montreal on both English and French radio stations (CJAD and CKAC) and also helped out the Canadian Paraplegic Association. That sense of commitment to the community by club members is something Mabel Hubbard would have applauded. A sentiment that was also evident in a speech given by club founder, Doris Penfold, during her 1934-36 presidency, "It is plain that we represent a substantial unit, not only in our Company, but in our community... We can, moreover, as a club, become a real and very potent force for good in our community, but we must stand together... Why not join this group? Think of what could be accomplished if the whole 750 of us really worked for relief this winter."[4]

Over the next twenty years Mabel Hubbard Clubs were started at other Bell branches in Toronto, Hamilton, London, Quebec, St. Catherines, and Barrie. The clubs provided social, educational and sports programs of all kinds for Bell employees and their friends. Their community and welfare work ranged from sending children to summer camps, reading to children in hospital, providing hearing aids to underprivileged deaf children, and distributing food and toys to the needy. Their concern for the well being of others also began to stretch out beyond the community and even outside the country. In the 1960's the St. Catherine's Mabel Hubbard Club reached out to the peoples of Africa when they sent money to help Father Oswald Colussi as he worked among the lepers in Wau, Sudan. Father Colussi wrote many letters to the MHC members over the years thanking them for their continued help and support in his fight to help the lepers. That same St. Catherine's club also adopted a girl in France by the name of Bernadette, sending her care packages and making sure she got a good start in life. They had tried to adopt a girl from the Northwest Territories but were told then that this was not possible.

When the Montreal branch celebrated its 25th anniversary in 1958, the honored guest was Mrs. Lillian Grosvenor Jones, Mabel Hubbard's granddaughter. Held at the Queen Elizabeth Hotel approximately 400 members were on hand to welcome Mrs. Jones - all members dressed in the fashions of the 1930's. Mrs. Jones expressed her appreciation of the Club's work with the deaf (providing hearing-aids for underprivileged deaf children) and also noted that her grandmother would have loved both the social and welfare projects of the club. "She was an artist, an excellent hostess, world traveler and social worker. Your fashion and beauty clinics would have fascinated her, for she loved beautiful clothes."[5]

By 1971 men were being admitted to the club and Dave Cochrane who worked in Montreal's accounting department became the first male member. For many more years the club continued with its work until sadly the club closed on December 23rd, 1994. Financial difficulties were cited as the reason for closure. The club no longer had the revenue to support its many activities and projects.

Mabel Hubbard's commitment to community was one of her most outstanding qualities. That the female Bell employees (and male to) chose her name to honor their club is testament to her legacy. When I look back over the history of the Mabel Hubbard Club it is truly remarkable the amount of time and energy these people put into their community. These women (and men) are to be commended for their contributions to our society and yet it's sad to note that so few people know of their existence. I hope my book will change that.

9. Mabel And Education

*T*he Canadian Home and School and Parent-Teacher Federation (CHSPTF) celebrated its 100th anniversary in 1995 and it was this very anniversary that initiated the writing of this book. As a member of the Home & School Association I wanted to know more about Mabel Hubbard Bell, our founder, and after much research discovered a rather remarkable woman.

Back in 1895 Mabel was instrumental in getting together a group of Baddeck parents to form a Parents Association that would concern itself with their children's' education, needs and welfare. She had witnessed such parental groups in the United States and saw immediately the benefits they could bestow upon the children, the teachers and the schools in Nova Scotia. Mabel made up her mind to set up an association in Baddeck and on December 18th, 1895 they met in the Academy building. This was the birth of the Canadian Home & School Federation! In Mabel Hubbard's times the needs were simple (charts, window blinds, maps etc.) but the basic issues concerning health, welfare and education have remained the same over the years. More than 100 years later Home and School Associations are working hard right across Canada to provide a better standard of life, education and well-being for all children.

The CHSPTF received its Letters Patent in 1951 and its mission statement is as follows: -

The Canadian Home & School, Parent-Teacher Federation is a federation of provincial and local parent-teacher groups which promotes the welfare of children and youth, raises the standards of home life, fosters cooperation between parents and teachers, fosters high ideals of citizenship, and, through education, promotes international peace and goodwill.

At the CHSPTF's annual meeting in 1996, held in Seebe, Alberta, it was unanimously passed that the name be shortened and changed to the "Canadian Home & School Federation" (CHSF).

Two years after Mabel had organized the very first Home &

School in Canada the PTA (Parent-Teacher Association) held its first official meeting in the United States. The PTA of the United States and the CHSPTF of Canada are sister organizations that both concern themselves with children, their education, homelife, welfare and the connections between all those factors to promote a better and brighter future for all our children.

The PTA started out as the National Congress of Mothers in 1897, became the National Congress of Mothers and Parent-Teacher Associations in 1908 and changed its name again in 1924 to the National Congress of Parents and Teachers. Today they are simply known as the PTA.

Although not a founder of the PTA, Mabel did take an active interest in the association's beginnings with her daughters. The first National Congress of Mothers met in Washington D.C. February 17th, 18th, and 19th, 1897. A full and wide-ranging program was set out for those three days and the event was well publicized across the United States via magazines and a letter writing campaign to various clergymen and leading women's clubs. Mabel and her daughters were among the two thousand that attended and heard speeches on such topics as, Mother and Child of the Primitive World, What Kindergarten Means to Mothers, Day Nurseries, Parental Reverence as Taught in the Hebrew Homes, and The Value of Music in the Development of Character. A reception was also held for the delegates by Mrs. Cleveland at the White House.

THE ORIGINAL MINUTES

On the 18th of December 1895 a number of Ladies met in the Academy Building, having for their object the organization of a Parents Association for connection with Baddeck Schools of Baddeck. Miss G. McCurdy was asked to take the chair.

Mrs. Macaskill was asked to act as secretary for the afternoon.

The By-Laws & Constitution --- previously prepared --- were read by the Secretary. After a short discussion a motion was made by Mrs. E.W. MacCurdy, seconded by Mrs. K.J. MacKay that the Constitution & By-Laws be adopted as a whole. Motion carried unanimously. The following officers were then elected for the year.

President	Miss McCurdy
Treasurer	Mrs. D. McDonald
Secretary	Mrs. M.G. Macaskill

The elected President then read a letter from Mrs. A. G. Bell highly recommending the organization of a Parents Association & enclosing a check for $25.00 to be added to their funds. Miss McPhee, Principal of the Academy also read a letter from W. McKay, Superintendent of Education, expressing his regret at not being able to accept the kind invitation sent from the Ladies of Baddeck to be present at the School Entertainment held on the 17th and also highly approving of the efforts put forth by the Ladies in endeavouring to help promote the cause of Education in Baddeck.

While the Ladies were discussing what they could do at the present time in aid of the school, the principal informed the meeting that a young man was waiting at the door to make known to them the immediate requirements of the school. On being allowed admittance Mr. John McLennon read a paper outlining those requirements.

As funds were too small to supply all the requirements it was moved and seconded and passed that the following should be provided for at once. 3 modulators, 3 colour charts, window blinds for all the rooms and Bio-Hemisphere maps. Also books and oil cloth for map protection.

Meeting then adjourned to meet in the Academy January 7th, 1896

M.G. Macaskill
Secretary

Mabel took a great interest in the education of her daughters and her grandchildren. A well educated woman herself she knew well the benefits of a good all round education and the importance of active participation by parents in that endeavour. Never more was this evident as when Mabel and her husband took an interest in the Montessori School system.

Mabel Hubbard first read of the Montessori system of education in McClure's Magazine. Several articles appeared during 1911 written by Tozier. Both Mabel and her husband felt that this new approach to education was ideal for their grandchildren. The "individual approach" and the attention given to different children learning at different rates appealed to them....

> that human development does not occur in a steady,
> linear ascent but in a series of formative planes
>
> that the complete development of human beings is
> made possible by their tendencies to certain
> universal actions in relation to their environment
>
> that this interaction with the environment is most
> productive in terms of the indidviual's development
> when it is self-chosen and founded upon individual
> interest.[1]

Mabel decided to visit a Montessori School in New York to see such a system in action and then returned to D.C. to set up a second Montessori School for her grandchildren. She liked what she saw. As the Bells spent a great deal of time in Baddeck during the summer and falls months she also decided to set up a school there. It was the very first Montessori School in Canada (see chapter four).

Because of who they were the Bells had many influential friends with many connections and were able to well publicize the Montessori System of Education. They garnered a lot of support within the D.C. community. So great was the interest that a Montessori Education Association was established. As an association their aim was to promote the Montessori method throughout the United States and establish more schools. A Montessori America Committee had also been formed earlier which organized the first international training course in Rome for would-be Montessori teachers. Sixty-seven women set sail from the United States to take the course in Rome under Maria Montessori herself.

Mabel, as first President of the Montessori Education Association (MEA), worked very hard for the cause speaking with parent groups, obtaining a new building for their D.C. school and also producing a MEA News Bulletin. A year after Mabel had opened the second Montessori school in America another 100 such schools opened across the country. The Montessori Method was well-known now and became subject to much criticism and was the subject of much controversy. People began to wonder outloud if this new approach to education was the right one.

When Maria Montessori returned to the US in the winter of 1913, Mabel arranged a huge reception for her at their D.C. home on December 6th. The purpose of Montessori's trip was to see for herself first hand how the students and teachers were performing in her schools. That first encounter came at the D.C. school on Kalorama Road. She was impressed!

On the evening of December 6th after a lecture at the Masonic Temple some 400 guests gathered at the Bell home to honour their guest Maria Montessori. Mabel wore lavender satin and lace that evening. As always she was an elegant hostess and had planned the evening with great care and her usual eye for great detail. Anybody who was anybody in D.C. society circles was at that reception.

All seemed well with the Montessori method but only a year later (1914) people were becoming disenchanted with the lady herself and the system. Mabel's son-in-law, Gilbert Grosvenor, an original member of the MEA was finding it difficult to have dealings with Maria Montessori who was becoming very domineering and lacking in the ability, as he put it, to know just who her friends were. He wanted Mabel to retire as President of the MEA.

Montessori had become insistent on overseeing every single aspect of work done in her "name" etc. She would make accusations of being "exploited" when not consulted and thought people were cheating her out of money. When she returned to the US in 1914 she handed over a copy of the General Regulations for Formation of an Authorized Montessori Society to Mabel and the MEA. In it she stated that only teachers trained after 1913 could now legally teach in Montessori schools - in effect making most if not all of the teachers unfit to teach. Mabel and the Washington group did not take well to this lack of confidence in their association. Mabel Bell and association members had worked hard to promote and build the schools across the United States and they were reluctant to dissolve their own association. They were now 700 members strong in D.C. They also felt that a show of disharmony between them and Dr. Montessori would not bode well for the movement in America. Maria Montessori also did not like the bulletins that Mabel was publishing - because she could not check and approve each and every item in them. Mabel was just trying to promote and popularize the qualities of the Montessori method and instead of being praised she was having criticism thrown in her face. It was a big blow for Mabel and all her colleagues. When Montessori founded a new organization called the National Montessori Promotion Fund, the MEA decided to dissolve itself in the fall of 1916. They cited too many overlaps between the two organizations and the fact that the new one had more support and money as reasons for their termination. Mabel did however become a member of the Fund's Board of Trustees. By February of 1917 the movement was falling apart and Mabel was told that her job had been done and she was no longer needed. So ended Mabel's involvement with the Montessori Educational System.

As a parent Mabel knew the importance of the home and school connection and always took a keen and active interest in the education of her children and her grandchildren. Her sense of community, commitment, love and caring were perhaps the greatest gifts she gave her daughters and their children.

10. My thoughts on Mabel Hubbard

Mabel Hubbard had a great sense of history. Whether she acquired this through her own insatiable appetite for historical works or whether it was a sixth sense, she nevertheless knew she was part of it. When fiancé, Alexander Graham Bell, was busy working on the telephone she knew it would bring greatness to mankind. How do we know all this? Simply because Mabel kept all her letters and those of her husband and family and insisted that they not be destroyed so that that they could stand as a written history of the times. Mabel, Mr. Bell, and all the family wrote many long and detailed letters, which are still available today for all to see and gain knowledge from. These letters not only let us delve into their private lives but also do record the history of the times. Mabel had the forethought to keep these "records" for future generations.

Mabel also possessed a great sense of "community" which I believe was instilled in her by her parents, in particular her father, Gardiner Greene Hubbard. As a founding father of the city of Cambridge, Massachusetts, U.S.A., Mr. Hubbard set a fine example to Mabel on how to help one's community by getting involved and making long-lasting contributions. Mabel did just that when she set up the Cottage Industries in Baddeck, Nova Scotia, started a library there, and the Young Ladies Club, brought in the first Victoria Order of Nurses and organized the very first Home & School, not to mention the first Montessori school in Canada. She organized parents in Washington too and became very active with the Montessori Educational Association, Women's Suffrage, and the National Congress of Mothers. This sense of community was also passed onto her daughter, Elsie Grosvenor, who led the fight for women's rights as an officer in the Washington D.C. branch of the National American Women's Suffrage Association. Elsie also became one of the driving forces behind the highly successful National Geographic. Children do learn by example!

Although she did not attend college or university, Mabel was a well-educated woman. A combination of reading, travelling and social standing made for a well-rounded intelligent Victorian woman. She was bright and smart beyond her years and what is most amazing about all of this is that she was handicapped. Mabel was deaf. Despite her deafness Mabel became a caring, influential and wealthy woman. A woman of great foresight who gave so much of herself to others and for the benefit of others.

For the greater part of her life Mabel was isolated from other deaf children/people by choice. She did not want to have deaf friends, or associate with deaf people. She did not want her children to have deaf friends. When her husband, Alexander Graham Bell, spent any time with deaf children she became angry and resentful. Perhaps, though, this self-denial and this unwillingness to associate with other deaf people is what actually helped her fit into a "regular" society. She was not an outcast and as we know she became an excellent lip-reader and orator. Mabel did not want to be treated differently just because she was deaf and perhaps this is what made her fit in and become fully integrated into society.

Later in life she did acknowledge it was selfish of her to want to deny her husband his involvement with the deaf. It was after all the love of his life and always came before his inventing. When her father died and she saw all that he had done for the deaf she did become more involved with deaf people via her written works on lip-reading and with the actual schools for the deaf.

Mabel was after all, just a human being who happened to be deaf and that should not make her less capable or less intelligent than anyone else. This was a point that Mr. Bell would make often when talking to people about the education of the deaf.

I think one of the things I admired most about Mabel was her tenacity. Although handicapped she never felt "trapped" in a world that in Victorian times was too quick to shun and label deaf people and send them off to the nearest asylum. She always knew what she wanted and went after it. She was not brash or arrogant about anything and her manner was always that of kindliness and propriety. She never gave up on anything she attempted and her thirst for knowledge, like that of her husband, was insatiable. She loved to read and she loved to travel and then she loved to pass on this acquired knowledge to others.

Mabel Hubbard was a pioneer, a trailblazer and together with her husband and her parents made the world a better place for deaf people through education and community action.

For me Mabel personified all that Home & Schoolers stand for. She was a caring mother and grandmother, an active community volunteer and always gave great forethought to future generations. She recognized that parents are their children's first teachers and she knew that when parents took an interest in their children's education it led to positive and successful experiences for the children. She knew it was important to be active, informed, responsible and supportive and that the partnership between home and school was an important one. Whether she knew she was a hero of sorts I don't know but she certainly made a difference during her time on this earth and all of it positive and worthwhile contributions. Her life story speaks for itself and for me it was a joy to research and write.

Important Dates

1857　November 25th, Mabel Hubbard born in Cambridge, Mass., USA.

1863　Mabel contracted Scarlet Fever - became deaf

1867　Mabel spoke at Massachusetts State Legislature Mabel's sister Marian died at age 2

1873　Mabel met Mr. Bell for the first time (had some speech lessons with him)

1874　In the Fall Mabel gave her first formal dance

1875　November 25th/Thanksgiving - Mabel and Bell got engaged - also Mabel's 18th birthday

1876　March - US Patent No. 174,465 was registered Patent for the basic telephone

1877　July 9th - Bell Telephone Company founded July 11th - Mabel and Bell married at Brattle Street home in Cambridge August 4th　　-　Mabel and Alec set sail for England

1878　May 8th - daughter Elsie May was born in London, England. Fall - Mabel, Alec and Elsie returned to North America

1880　February 15th - daughter Marian "Daisy" born in Washington, D.C.

1881　August 15th - son Edward born prematurely survived only a few short hours

1883　November 17th - son Robert born but survived only minutes

1885　Summer - discovered Baddeck, Nova Scotia, Canada July 4th - Mabel's sister Roberta died of tuberculosis

1886　Mabel's sister Gertrude died of tuberculosis

1887　January - fire at D.C. home at 1500 Rhode Island Ave

1891　Washington Club officially named in D.C. October 10th - Mabel founded the Young Ladies Club of Baddeck in Nova Scotia, Canada

1893　Beinn Bhreagh Hall completed in Baddeck, Nova Scotia, Canada

1894　Mabel wrote paper on speech reading (lip-reading)
　　　　Mabel established the Home Industries of Baddeck

1895　December 18th - Mabel founded the Canadian Home and School

1897　February - First National Congress of Mothers held in Washington, D.C. December 11th - Mabel's father, Gardiner Greene　　Hubbard died

1898 Mabel brought the first Victorian Order of Nurses (VON) to Baddeck with help from friend Lady Aberdeen

1900 October 23rd - daughter Elsie married Gilbert Grosvenor in London, England

1902 Mabel became a grandmother - first grandchild Melville Grosvenor

1905 April - daughter Daisy married David Fairchild in Washington, D.C.

1907 October 1st - Mabel financed the Aerial Experiment Association (AEA) and became the first woman patron of aviation

1909 March 31st - AEA dissolved October - Mabel's mother, Gertrude Hubbard died in a car accident

1911 VON closed down in Baddeck - lack of funds

1912 Mabel established a Montessori School in D.C. home
Mabel established first Montessori School in Canada in Baddeck, Nova Scotia

1913 April - Montessori Educational Association (MEA) was founded. Mabel became its first President

1917 Mabel wrote "Women of America" appeal for conscription in Washington, D.C.

1919 Montessori School in D.C. was closed

1921 Mabel's lifelong friend and former teacher, Mary True, died.

1922 August 2nd - husband Alexander Graham Bell died in Baddeck, Nova Scotia, Canada. Young Ladies Club of Baddeck was renamed the Alexander Graham Bell Club

1923 January 3rd - Mabel Hubbard died at daughter Daisy's home in Maryland, USA August 7th - Mabel's ashes buried alongside husband, Alexander Graham Bell in Baddeck

1933 March 14th - Mabel Hubbard Club founded by Bell women employees in Montreal, Canada

1958 Lillian Grosvenor Jones (Mabel's granddaughter) attended 25th Anniversary of the Mabel Hubbard Club in Montreal

1994 December 23rd - Mabel Hubbard Club dissolved due to lack of funds

1995 Canadian Home and School Federation celebrated it's 100th Anniversary

Original Short Article That Inspired This Book

Who Was Mabel Hubbard?

By
Ann Bishundayal

Yes, just who was Mabel Hubbard? Any "true" Home & Schooler will tell you that she is the reason for our existence. Home & Schools began 100 years ago thanks to Mabel and other concerned parents just like her from Baddeck, Nova Scotia. But just who was she? Well....

Mabel Hubbard was born on November 25th, 1857 – the daughter of a wealthy Boston lawyer, Gardiner Greene Hubbard. At the age of five Mabel contracted Scarlet Fever, which left her deaf. She did learn how to read lips, but her father wanted much more for his daughter, and in the fall of 1873 Mabel became one of Alexander Graham Bell's pupils at the Boston School for Deaf Mutes. She was almost 16 at this time and decided from the first moment she laid eyes on Mr. Bell, that she did not like this tall, thin scruffy-looking man at all! Mabel was a bright and attractive young girl and a very good student. Ten years her senior, Mr. Bell enjoyed his sessions with Mabel and began to have very "special" feelings for her. The inevitable happened, and Mr. Bell fell in love with Miss Hubbard. It took him a year and a half to pluck up the courage to tell her so in a letter and to ask her to marry him. Mabel's reply was that she did like him (she was actually now quite fond of him), but that she did not love him.

Liking was enough for Alexander who pursued his lady love all the more during 1875. Mabel's father was not too happy about this as he was one of Mr. Bell's financial backers and wanted him to spend less time chasing his daughter and more time "inventing". Finally, though, on November 25th, 1875 Mabel and Alexander became engaged. She was now 18. They were married on July 11th, 1877 just two days after the Bell Telephone Company was formed. A year later their daughter was born (Elsie May), with a second daughter (Marion Daisy) arriving just two years later. In

1881 and again in 1883 Mabel gave birth to sons, both of whom died in early infancy.

Mr. and Mrs. Bell were now living in Washington D.C. In the summer of 1885 Mabel, Alexander, Elsie and Daisy visited Baddeck, Nova Scotia. They fell in love with the place, decided to buy property there and a year later moved into a small cottage at Crescent Grove, Baddeck Bay. Several years later (1892/93) they built a new home on Red Point called Beinn Bhreagh (Gaelic for "beautiful mountain") overlooking Bras D'Or Lake. Many people called it the Bell Palace, it was so huge!

Mabel loved her new home. She loved being with people and entertained a lot in her new "palace"! There were always guests visiting, special suppers and afternoon teas. Mabel also shared her husband's love of experimenting and inventing. She even invested a lot of her own money in many of his ventures and carried on with his projects after his death.

In 1894 Mrs. Mabel Hubbard Bell wrote a paper on speech (lip) reading, which was published in over ten different countries. Then, on December 18th, 1895, Mabel assisted in organizing the "Parents' Association of Baddeck" after researching similar organizations in Washington D.C. and other parts of the States. One hundred years later Home & Schools are still going strong across Canada. Thank you Mabel! Her husband died on August 2nd, 1922. She held his hand to the very end. Mabel missed him very much and died just five months later on January 3rd, 1923. They are buried next to one another on their beloved "beautiful mountain".

So now you know who Mabel Hubbard is! The next time you hear someone talking about Alexander Graham Bell, you can say: "Oh yes, wasn't he the husband of Mrs. Mabel Hubbard?!"

HAPPY 100TH ANNIVERSARY

Canadian Home & School, Parent-Teacher Federation from all at

ELIZABETH BALLANTYNE SCHOOL

AMERICAN ASSOCIATION TO PROMOTE THE TEACHING
OF SPEECH TO THE DEAF

FOURTH SUMMER MEETING,

Chautauqaua, N. Y., July 1894

(Proceedings issued in sections)

"Further contribution to the study of that
subtile art which may inable one with an
observant eie to heare what any man
speaks by moving of the lips."
(Bulwer 1648)
by
Mrs. Alexander Graham Bell,

The Teaching of Speech-reading To Adults
By
Miss Sarah Allen Jordan,

Speech-Reading
By
Miss Susan E. Bliss,

And

Speech-Reading
By
Miss Mabel Ellery Adams.

ROCHESTER:
Western New York Institution for Deaf-Mutes
1894

*W*hen President Gillett asked me to write a paper on speech-reading for the American Association I said I did not see what I could say about it. Carrying on conversation by word of mouth is as natural and as easy to me as to any hearing person. Of course I speak, and of course, being deaf and therefore unable to read speech by ear, I read it by eye, and there is nothing more to be said. As to the how – does any one take thought how they see, and hear, and move? Why then should I examine any more closely the mechanism by which I see lips move and translate the movements into speech – than the mechanism by which I see trees move, and become conscious that the wind is blowing from the east to the west? Both are processes of deduction from past experience and knowledge. So also it is by deduction from past experiences and knowledge that the hearing person comprehends a certain variety of sound as speech. But the process by which he accomplishes this is a very great mystery to me. I wish President Gillett would explain to me how he understands speech. How much of the process is mental, and how much mechanical? How many years did it take him to learn to comprehend speech by ear, and was it difficult at first? How does he know that one sound that can be represented by a sharper pointed zig-zag line than another is one word, instead of the other? I am afraid President Gillett might find some difficulty in making this clear to me, and I know I find great difficulty in trying to explain how I hear by eye. So much indeed, that I have been on the point several times of giving up the attempt in despair. The more smoothly a piece of machinery runs the less the operator thinks or knows about it. It is only when it gets rusty and refuses to work that the operator has to study its mechanism in order to remedy the defect, and thus becomes acquainted with its method of working. Thus it has been with my speech-reading machinery. Generally it works so easily I do not pay any attention to it at all. It is only since President Gillett did me the honour to ask me for my ideas on the subject that I have been trying to take this machinery of min apart and study its mechanism. I submit now the results and also, though with diffidence a few thoughts generally upon what the quaint old 17th century philosopher, John Bulwer, so aptly describes as "that Subtile Art which may inable one with an observant Eie to Heare what any man speaks by the moving of his lips."

I think, perhaps, if I could remember both having once heard, and then losing my hearing, and the processes by which I learned a new way of communicating with my friends, I might have less difficulty in explaining both how I did it, and the nature of the difficulties I, and all the other students of the "Subtile Art" have to overcome. As it happened, however, I was so young when the illness which deprived me of my hearing occurred – it was severe – my convalescence was so slow, and the consequent mental weakness so great, that I not only cannot remember ever having heard, but cannot even recollect having been in a materially different position as regards articulation and speech-reading from one I have occupied for so many years. Of course, I could have spoken and read speech as well as a child as I did later, but I cannot recollect being conscious of any difficulty in communicating with my friends. More, I do not remember that the fact of my deafness was ever borne in upon me then. Of course, I knew it, as one knows the sun is shining, or that it is cloudy, without its making any impression upon the mind. My strongest feeling, as regards myself and my sisters, was that I was eighteen months older than the eldest, and therefore, very much wiser and more experienced.

I presume the reason why I remember nothing of my first steps in speech-reading and articulation is due to the long period of mental and physical feebleness which followed my illness. My mother says that for many months I took no interest in anything and seemed to have no wants to express, and the baby speech I had previously possessed seemed entirely gone. During all that time my mother was working, planning and striving, by every means in her power to give me back the speech I had lost, and to make me read her lips. She talked to me long before I cared to talk back, and gradually, I suppose, both language and the ability to read speech came together with increasing mental and physical health. The process must have been gradual, and I must have learned to speak and read lips together, for I remember nothing of all this, and it seems to me obvious that if I could speak much more, and sooner than I could understand others, or vice versa, there must have been a disproportion between the two powers which would have left an impression on my mind. However this may be, it remains true that my earliest recollections are of being able to talk, and of understanding what was said to me, at least sufficiently well to satisfy all my requirements.

I remember no stormy outbursts of passion, such as I believe are too often consequent on the inability of a deaf child to make his wants known. Looking back now, it seems to me that whatever method my mother, and the young, inexperienced girl of twenty who assisted her, pursued in my instruction, must have been the true and natural one, simply because it has left no trace on my memory. All natural processes of growth are gradual and imperceptible, there are no violent shocks and sudden changes such as leave a mark on the memory. It is the unnatural methods of instruction, that by demanding unnatural, and therefore painful efforts from the child, leave marks of the work on his mind. You may think that I am theorizing upon a subject about which I, not being a teacher can know nothing, but I have in mind the one item in the plan of my instruction, which I do remember, and which I believe impressed itself on my memory just because it was unnatural. This was a daily drill in writing from dictation sentences, which our teacher read from a book. My sisters, with whom I was educated, shared in this drill, and I do not remember objecting very strongly to it, but it was most slow and irksome work, and I always remembered it was the one lesson I did not like. Well, to day it is no uncommon occurrence for my husband to talk to me perhaps half an hour at a time of something in which he is interested. It may be on the latest geographical discoveries; Sir Robert Ball's "Story of the Sun"; the latest phase of the Hawaiian trouble, - some abstruse scientific problem in gravitation, - anything and everything. Very rarely do I have to ask him to repeat, and at the end I would be ready to back myself to give the substance of what he had said, almost word for word, as well as any hearing person. But it is absolutely and utterly impossible for Mr. Bell to sit down and read me the shortest paragraph from the simplest book, and have me understand him without the greatest difficulty and strain.

I have often wondered why this should be so, and tried to detect where the difference cam in, but without success, it is so slight and imperceptible. Mr. Bell is a good and expressive reader; yet there is a change in his manner of reading or of "holding forth," as the expressive slang phrase has it, which makes all the difference between ease and difficulty of comprehension. And what is true of Mr. Bell is true of every one with whom I have held communication. I have therefore learned to read lips, not because of the drill in dictation, but in spite of it. I am convinced, therefore, that the drill was a mistake, unnecessary, a waste of time, and that it is not to be recommended as a means to the acquisition of the "Subtile Art."

With this exception, I cannot remember that any special exercises were set to teach me speech-reading. I just grew into it naturally – just as a hearing child grows into the knowledge of hearing speech – by perpetual practice. Every one spoke to me – no one made any signs and I cannot remember making any, or wanting to make any. I observed that whenever my mother's visitors came to call they talked to one another so fast that I could not understand them, and that I couldn't talk as fast myself – but I was quite satisfied that the ability to do both would come by and by with long dresses – and, meanwhile, I and my sisters played "visitors" and talked gibberish as fast as we could, and were satisfied.

But while emphasizing the fact that my acquisition of speech-reading was a process of growth, to me perfectly natural, I would not be understood as claiming that no special effort was made to teach me. On the contrary, few children have had more care and anxious thought bestowed on the best means of instructing them – but I do claim that my mother and teacher – whether by accident or great wisdom and good judgement, happened to hit upon what was for me the best possible method of instruction – and the proof of this lies in the fact that I, the child, was conscious of nothing forced or painful in my growth into understanding. I am not the best possible speech-reader, but this does not militate against the merit of the method employed for reasons that I will explain later, when I come to describe the qualifications for speech-reading.

The method of the instruction pursued by my mother and teacher – pioneers in a new world of effort, as truly Columbus himself – was essentially the same as that pursued with my two younger hearing sisters. In fact, we were taught together and I remember no difference being made between us. Very early books were placed in my hands and I became passionately fond of reading. I did not care to romp and play out of doors; all I wanted was to curl up in some quiet corner and read – all day long if allowed. My father's library was well stocked and I had almost free range. When eleven years old I delighted in reading such books as Jane Porter's "Scottish Chiefs," and before I was thirteen I had read through with intense interest, Motley's "Rise of the Dutch Republic," most of Prescott's histories, several large volumes of the civil war – books of travel – as well as all the stories and novels I could get hold of. We went abroad for three years, when I was twelve, and my mother made me a point of giving me all the histories and historic novels she could find of the places we visited. I went through a good many books this way. Carlyle's "French Revolution" was the only book at which I rebelled, and when I made a list of the words I could not understand my mother did not insist, as they were pretty well beyond her own comprehension.

I have dwelt thus at length upon this reading of mine because upon it rests all my success in speech-reading

From the day my mother knew I would lose my hearing, to that on which she gave me into my husband's care, she was working and planning for her child – eagerly seizing every opportunity that promised advantage. Of all the good she did for me the greatest was when she taught me this love of reading and gave me the means to gratify it.

I have looked back over my life – I have taken apart my speech-reading apparatus – I have thought carefully over all my experiences – and the result at which I have arrived is that not only in success in speech-reading dependent upon reading – or, rather, on the extensive and intimate knowledge of language imparted by reading – but that speech-reading is impossible to any useful extent without it.

The "observant Eie can Heare" part, but this, which our 17th century guide and philosopher thought essential to the knowledge of the "Subtile Art," Helen Keller, and others like her, have proved is not absolutely necessary. By carefully studying my daily practice in speech-reading throughout that it is essentially and primarily a mental art, the mechanical act of reading or feeling the movements of the speaker's lips forming, - although a necessary, - yet but a small part of the whole.

Speech-reading is the systematized result of practice:-

1. In selecting the right word from a large assortment of possible words presented to the eye or hand:-

2. In the power of grasping the meaning of what is said as a whole, from possible a few words, or even parts of those words recognized here and there.

1st.   There is a very large number of words which are alike to the eye. In fact, it is possible to see resemblances between almost every word and a dozen others. Consequently, the eye, the finger, alone cannot determine which of a dozen possible words is the one used by the speaker. It is therefore necessary first, that there should be an intimate knowledge of a large number of words, from which to select the probable word, and second, that the habit of making the selection should be so well established that it could be done instantaneously and automatically. In perfect speech-reading there is no more conscious effort in this selection than in the act of winking.

2nd.   In consequence of the large number of words that are alike to the eye, the art of speech-reading consists in seeking to grasp the meaning of what is said, as a whole, rather than in wasting time trying to decipher the words one by one. By making sure of a word, here and there, by the method shown above, the trained mind is able to fill the blanks between, and to spring instantaneously to a clear realization of what is being said. This, too, in perfect speech-reading is automatic and unconscious and the mind of the speech-reader keeps pace with the speaker, so that it might appear as if the speech-reader really read the words mechanically – one by one – from the lips. I might often be led into this belief myself – I can generally follow my intimate friends so easily and rapidly, - but I am undeceived by finding that occasionally my friend has finished speaking without my having understood a word. Then before the word "What?" is fairly out of mouth, the whole sentence will flash into my mind complete, word for word, like a flash of light projected into darkness, and is as apparently without volition on my part as the distant flash from the lighthouse.

Do I make it clear? I don't assert that it is impossible to read word by word, - mechanically, from the speaker's lips. That is quite possible, but it is the slowest, most uninteresting and the most difficult method of speech-reading and it is only possible when the speaker articulates with unnatural slowness and deliberation, and is no more accurate than the other. For, adding together the power of grasping meanings as wholes, and the habit of selecting the correct words from the knowledge of resemblances, the result in perfect speech-reading is the understanding of every word spoken, as surely and a thousand times more rapidly than by the mechanical word by word deciphering.

It has the further advantage of allowing the speaker to speak almost as rapidly and indistinctly as usual. For, as every one knows, few, even of the most precise speakers, give to each word its full value. Words are more or less slurred over and run together, so that really there are few properly pronounced words for the speech-reader to see. Consequently, if one is to go out into the world and read the ordinary careless half-uttered speech of the generality of mankind it is necessary to cultivate the habit of going as straightly as possible to the point, and bothering as little as may be about the exact words used. Ninety-nine times out of a hundred this is all that is required, or, I venture to say, is remembered the next moment by a hearing person. My practice is to allow a talker to go on with what he is saying, even if not one word is understood, in the hope that before the end a word or two may be recognized which will, as it were, throw a flood of light upon the whole speech, rendering past words intelligible. In this way, it is often possible for me to understand the long story or speech of a person whose short remarks are hard to follow.

Strangers in general and people unaccustomed to conversation with speech-readers, sometimes seem to think that the converse of this is true; that they must talk in short, jerky sentences, using as few words as possible. Of course, this, by reducing to a minimum the number of words out of which the speech-reader may hope to cull one or two with which to decipher the meaning, only increases the difficulty of comprehension.

Words of many syllables are more readily understood than short ones, for the same reason that sentences, as wholes, are more comprehensible than single words, there is more to take hold of.

Ordinary questions and conversational remarks, being not only short, composed of few words, - but these few words of the shortest, fewest syllables, might be almost incomprehensible but ·for the natural expressions of the face which generally accompany them.

Hearing people depend on these facial expressions to an extent that is, perhaps, not realized until some humorous fellow delivers himself of a joke with a perfectly serious face and in a flat voice. The very essence of the fun to him is to observe the bewilderment depicted on the faces of his hearers, the voluntary pause, hesitation, longer with some, shorter with others, before his meaning breaks upon them, and the laugh goes round. It is impossible to open a novel, a biography, or hardly a daily newspaper without coming across commendatory references to a speaker's expressive face, the suggestive modulations of his voice, or, complaints of the difficulty of following the ideas of a monotonous speaker. What does all this mean if not that hearing people, possessors of a language made by themselves, and by them adapted as perfectly as may be to their own convenience, yet find it necessary to invent some other method of making a speaker's ideas clear.

They have invented the rising inflection of the voice for questions; falling ones for answers or assertions till the fortunate beings can almost grasp the speaker's remarks without the trouble of listening to his words. Every hearing person makes liberal use of smiles and frowns, the stern, or the gentle mien to enforce his meaning. So important is the proper use of these aids to comprehension considered, that schools of oratory have been established for their study, in which inflection of the voice, turn of the head or the hand, the lifting of an eyebrow receives due and careful consideration.

And all this for the benefit of hearing people with a language of their own making!!

The speech-reader is, therefore, but following the usage of his hearing fellow in availing himself of the only one of these adventitious aids to comprehension open to him; namely, study of the expressions of the face. This study becomes quite as instinctive and unconscious with him as with hearing persons, and by its aid many obscure questions or short remarks are elucidated.

I know at once by the speaker's natural involuntary glance whether a question is being asked, or a casual, unimportant remark being uttered. I bend at once my energies to mastering the question, and if I cannot understand it in one form, I beg that it be repeated in another; the remark, if I fear a tussle to understand, I let slide.

Fancy the feelings of a shy, innocent stranger at seeing a speech-reader struggle laboriously to comprehend some careless remark about the weather! How she wishes she hadn't said anything; how quickly she edges off from the embarrassing person, and how she carefully avoids further conversation with her. How much better for the speech-reader to encourage her to talk on and on, until, at last, words are recognized to which the speech-reader can reply, and conversation become established.

The habit of thus seizing the resemblances of words and springing to the realization of what is said as a whole, is, of course the result of long training and practice. With me, this training began from the very beginning, and the habit was formed unconsciously, and I am only made aware of its existence when struggling with the difficulty of understanding a stranger. I have no doubt, however, that this habit could be systematically cultivated. It should not take long for one possessing a good knowledge of language and a quick, bright mind to develop into a fair speech-reader. I noticed at the last two meetings of the American Association that several of our brightest teachers were speech-readers; some hearing members of my family have learned to read speech pretty well without much effort, and I recommend its study strongly to hearing people. I believe there is a great future before it when its adaptability to various purposes becomes better understood. For instance, it is a great convenience in a noisy place, where it is "almost impossible to hear one's self speak."

If I needed proof that speech-reading is essentially an intellectual exercise demanding good vernacular knowledge of language I should find it in my experience with German.

For six months, at one time, I lived in a German boarding school with only one friend with whom to talk English. Before the end of that time, I could read the German speech by eye nearly as readily as the English, and it was but rarely that anyone had to write off a German sentence for me. This was many years ago, and since then my opportunities for talking and listening to Germans have been few. I find now that when I meet a German friend and try to carry on a conversation in German, I cannot do it at first. I can put together a few German phrases to express my own ideas, but I cannot decipher the movements of the speaker's lips. Why? I find it is because the German vocabulary at my command is too small to allow me to select from it some words that may be the words my friend is using. I find myself consciously and painfully running over my small stock of possible words, much as a miser over his store of coin, and the chances are infinitely against my having the right word. This would be disheartening but that I have found by experience that by reading German books for a while, steeping my brains in German, as it were, so that I think in German, and see in German, it becomes comparatively easy to catch the German words on my friends lips.

Many people have the idea that in order to be understood by a speech-reader they must speak more slowly, and open their mouths wider. Up to a certain point, and with some people, - not all, - I find it true that slower and more distinct articulation is an advantage, but beyond that point slowness of utterance is a distinct hinderance to comprehension, while the unnatural opening of the mouth is almost prohibitive of conversation. In the first case, the speech-reader's mind, accustomed to run rapidly, is apt to assume, either that there must be more words in each slow movement of the mouth than appears, and be thrown off the track, or forced to linger over and study each word forgets the previous ones, and confused by a mass of details, fails to grasp the full meaning.

In the second case, the widely opened mouth, showing parts of words not usually perceived, so changes their accustomed appearance as to render them unintelligible.

There are no two faces in the world exactly alike, and every person has his own peculiar way of speaking. In some the peculiarity is greater than in others, and the difficulty of comprehension is increased, so much so, that at first it may seem utterly impossible to make head or tail of what is seen. I am, however, inclined to believe that there is no speech so indistinct which a first-class speech-reader can not master after a while.

It would be hard to say what makes intelligibility to a speech-reader. A great deal of lip action may be difficult to understand, yet too little is equally detrimental. Again, the lip action may be good and yet some peculiarity of the tongue or teeth or of pronunciation render the speech difficult to read. Moustaches, if not too heavy, make little difference one way or another, except at night under a hanging light, when of course, they shadow the mouth. I think, take it all in all, that if there are no abnormal peculiarities of the organs of articulation, or of pronunciation, it depends principally on the speech-reader whether the speech is intelligible or not. Practice makes perfect, and although I have met many people whom I could not understand I am not convinced that I could not have understood most of them in time, - given the opportunity and the desire to become accustomed to their peculiarity of speaking.

Besides, I do not account myself in any way, a first-class speech-reader, and people whom I find difficult to understand, others might find easy.

Bulwer's "Art " is as truly an art as any other. There are grades in it, as in others, and special talents are required to attain great proficiency in it. An active, alert mind constantly on the qui vive to receive impressions; keen as a razor in reaching the salient point of things; bright sharp eyes that see everything and let nothing escape, are qualifications for attaining a high degree of proficiency in the art, and these, however many other nice things I may have, are not mine. The best system of education without special talent will not create a Michael Angelo, but it may make a very good, practical artist, who can do sufficiently good work to support himself and his family in comfort. So, without any special inherent fitness for speech-reading, I have attained sufficient skill to serve all practical purposes. My father and mother, my husband and children, my relatives and friends, and my servants, all talk to me, and I at least have never felt that there was any bar to the fullest and freest communication between the immediate members of my family and myself. The occasions when one of them has to use paper and pencil are of the rarest, perhaps once a month, to spell some unfamiliar word or name. With less intimate friends and business people, communication, of course, is much more restricted, and often I get one of my daughters to act as interpreter. I might, of course, use pen and paper, but the strange part of my experience is that no one will take the trouble to write to me if it can possibly be avoided. If an interpreter is not at hand, the speaker will prefer to repeat again and again, until my patience is exhausted, and I will insist on the pencil and paper, which reluctantly used, will be dropped the instant I show signs of understanding without them. This experience is universal. Ladies and gentlemen, trades people and servants – all regard writing as a nuisance, to be avoided as much as possible.

In conclusion, I would offer, as the contribution of a disciple of John Bulwer, the following:-

1.That speech-reading is essentially an intellectual exercise; the mechanical part performed by the eye or finger in tracing the movements of the mouth, although necessary, is entirely subsidiary.

2. That speech-reading is practically impossible without a good band readily available colloquial knowledge of vernacular language.

3.That while speech-reading is practically impossible without a vernacular knowledge of language, that alone is not sufficient. The mind has to be trained to use this knowledge instantly and automatically, and this training is only possible through constant and persistent practice.

4.That the aim of the speech-reader should be to grasp a speaker's meaning as a complete whole, and not attempt to decipher it word by word or even sentence by sentence.

5. That speech-readers should be encourage to take advantage of every possible aid to reach the speaker's meaning, such as any hearing person would employ in conversation with another; viz, - expressions of emotion, etc., and finally:-

6. That to those whom the doors of sound are closed the acquisition of the "Subtile Art which may inable one with an observant Eie to Heare what any man speaks by the movement of his lips" is worth, and well repays, every possible effort to attain.

References:

Chapter 2 - Enter Mr. Bell
1. Letter from Mabel G. Bell to Mr. Fred DeLand (Volta Bureau), September 21st, 1906. From collection at Alexander Graham Bell Association for the Deaf, Inc. Washington, D.C.
2. Ibid.
3. Ibid.
4. Letter from Alec(Alexander Graham Bell) to May(Mabel Hubbard), June 22/3, 1876, Philadelphia. From the collection at Alexander Graham Bell Association for the Deaf, Inc., Washington, D.C.

Chapter 3 - D.C. Days
1. Washington Post, March 21st, 1897.
2. Grosvenor, Gilbert H., First Lady of the National Geographic. National Geographic, 128(1), July 1965, p. 115.
3. Ibid., p. 116
4. Bell, Mrs. A. G., Further Contribution To The Study Of That Subtile Art Which May Inable One With An Observant Eie To Heare What Any Man Speaks By The Moving Of The Lips. Fourth Summer Meeting. American Association to Promote The Teaching of Spccch to the Deaf, July 1894.

Chapter 4 - Baddeck Beckons
1. MacKenzie, Mrs. M. H., Some Recollections of Dr. and Mrs Bell's Arrival in Baddeck. Presented to the Alexander Graham Bell Club, Nova Scotia. Actual date unknown - circa 1923.
2. Lindo, P.R., The Bells of Baddeck. Reprinted from Conservation Canada, 1978.
3. MacKenzie, Mrs. M. H., op. cit.
4. MacKenzie, Mrs. M. H., op. cit.
5. Bell, Mrs. A. G., letters to Bureau of Plant Introduction, U.S. Department of Agriculture, June 16th, 1920.

6.   Grosvenor, Mrs. G., Mrs. A.G. Bell - A Reminiscence. The Volta Review, 59(7), September, 1957, p. 303-4.

Chapter 5 - Mabel Takes On New Challenges
1.   McCarry, Charles, The Three Men Who Made The Magazine. National Geographic 174(3), September 1988. Centennial Issue 1888-1988, p. 289
2.   Grosvenor, Mrs. G., Mrs. A. G. Bell - a Reminiscence. The Volta Review, 59(7), September, 1957, p. 303-4.
3.   Letter from Mabel G. Bell to Helen Keller, July 15th, 1918.   From the collection at the Alexander Graham Bell Association for the Deaf, Inc. Washington, D.C.
4.   Letter from Mabel G. Bell to Mrs. Lyon, October 4th, 1921.   From the collection at the Alexander Graham Bell Association for the Deaf, Inc. Washington, D.C.
5.   Newark, New Jersey, "Evening News" - Mrs. Mabel Hubbard-Bell: An Illuminant of Genius, January 6th, 1923. Author unknown.

Chapter 6 - Contributions to Baddeck Community
1.   "Search For Yesterday", Baddeck Public Library. April, 1981.
2.   McDonald, Daniel.   Letter to Miss McKenzie, Superintendent, Victorian Order of Nurses, Ottawa. March 1st, 1910.
3.   Ibid.
4.   Rowe, Betty Hughes, The Lady of Beinn Bhreagh.   The Blue   Bell, February 1961. (A Bell Canada Publication)
5.   Ibid.

Chapter 7 - Young Ladies Club of Baddeck
1.   Toward, Lilias M., The Alexander Graham Bell Club, 1961.   Baddeck, Nova Scotia, Canada.

Chapter 8 - Mabel Hubbard Club
1.   Fletcher, J. R., Ladies Are You Listening ? Beaver Hall Club Bulletin, February 28th, 1933. (A Bell Canada Publication)
2.   Ibid.
3.   Young, Ruth (Baillie), speech by, Montreal 1954. Mabel

Hubbard Club 21st Anniversary. (Bell Canada Archives)

4. Penfold, Doris, speech by, Montreal, December 1935. (Bell Canada Archives)

5. Hughes, Betty. Bell News, Vol 4(12), June 11th, 1958. 400 MHC Members Hear A.G. Bell's Granddaughter at Annual Meeting.

Chapter 9 - Mabel and Education
1. Lillard, Paula Polk. Montessori Today. A Comprehensive Approach to Education from Birth to Adulthood, p. 4/5.

Bibliography

Bell, A G. Canadian Pathfinders Series. Town, Florida: Grolier Ltd., 1988.

Bell, A G. Inventor of the Telephone. Copp, Clarke, Pitman Ltd., 1991.

Bruce, Robert V. Bell:Alexander Graham Bell and the Conquest of Solitude. Cornell University Press, New York, 1990.

It's About Us - Handbook, Canadian Home & School, Parent-Teacher Federation (CHSPTF). 11th Edition, 1985.

Kramer, Rita. Maria Montessori : A Biography. G P Putnam's and Sons, New York, 1976.

Lillard, Paula Polk. Montessori Today. A Comprehensive Approach to Education From Birth to Adulthood. Schocken Books, New York, 1996.

Madder, Charles Vincent. History 1895-1963 Canadian Home & School, Parent-Teacher Federation (CHSPTF). Maracle Press Ltd., Oshawa, Ontario, 1963.

National Geographic Magazine, The. August 1956, Vol. CX Number 2. Alexander Graham Bell : Tribute to Genius by the Honorable Jean Lesage, p. 227-256.

National Geographic. July 1965, Vol. 128, No. 1. First Lady of the National Geographic by Gilbert Hovey Grosvenor, p. 101-121.

National Geographic. September 1988, Vol. 174, No. 3. 1888-1988 Centennial Issue Three Men Who Made the Magazine by Charles McCarry, p. 287-316. and Alexander Graham Bell by Robert V. Bruce, p. 358-385.

Overstreet, Harry and Bonaro. Where Children Come First - A Study of the PTA Idea. National Congress of Parents and Teachers, Chicago, Illinois, Third Edition 1958. Originally published 1949.

Preliminary Inventories, National Archives, USA # 66. Records of the Bureau of Plant, Industry, Soils, Agricultural Engineering. Compiled by Harold T. Pinkett, Washington, 1954.

Through The Years (From the Scrapbook of Mrs. Mears. The beloved originator of Founders Day) National Congress of Parents & Teachers, Washington, D.C. No date.

Toward, Lilias M. Mabel Bell : Alexanders' Silent Partner. Methuen Publications, Ontario, Canada, 1984.

Picture Credits

Bell Canada. Use of this material granted permission of Bell Canada Historical Collection, Montreal (Quebec), Canada.

Bishundayal, Ann J. (Les Productions Ann-Tone Productions)

Clemen, Lawrence Photography

Garvel Deaf Centre, Greenock, Scotland.

Grosvenor, Gilbert H. Collection of Alexander Graham Bell Photographs, Library of Congress, Washington, D.C.

Volta Bureau, Alexander Graham Bell Association for the Deaf Inc., Washington, D.C.

Special thanks to Judy Lawry Ball for her extensive research at the Library of Congress.

Acknowledgements

Special thanks to the following who made valuable contributions to the book :-

1. R. Fisher Hudson, Q.C., Baddeck, Nova Scotia, Canada
2. Helena A. Phillipson, Newton, Massachusetts, U.S.A.
3. Anna Nicholson, Baddeck, Nova Scotia, Canada
4. Francis X. Kearney, Randolph, Massachusetts, U.S.A.
5. Library of Congress, Washington, D.C., U.S.A.
6. Ian R. MacIntosh, Regional Librarian, Cape Breton Regional Library, Sydney, Nova Scotia, Canada.
7. Sharon Morrow, Public Relations, Alexander Graham BellNational Historical Site, Baddeck, Nova Scotia, Canada.
8. Judith Anderson, Librarian, Alexander Graham Bell Association for the Deaf, Washington, D.C., U.S.A.
9. Aynsley MacFarlane, Chief, Visitor Activities, Alexander Graham Bell National Historical Site,Baddeck, Nova Scotia, Canada.
10. Charles Bahne, Historian/Consultant, Cambridge, Massachusetts, U.S.A.
11. Dawn, Nova Scotia Tourist Information, Halifax, Nova Scotia, Canada.
12. Stephanie L. Taylor, Resident Fellow, Cambridge Historical Society, Cambridge, Massachusetts, U.S.A.
13. James M. Vaughan, Jean McKenzie, Willie Lewis, University of Chicago Library, Chicago, Illinois, U.S.A.
14. Julie Crain, Research Correspondence, National Geographic Society, Washington, D.C., U.S.A.
15. Lorraine Croxen & France Jutras, Researchers, Bell Canada, Historical Collection, Montreal, Quebec, Canada.
16. Rita S. Macayeal, Archives II, Textual Reference Branch, National Archives at College Park, Maryland, U.S.A.
17. Ruth Mellor, Director of Communications, Victorian Order of Nurses for Canada, Ottawa, Ontario, Canada.
18. Pamela Q.J. Andre, Director, National Agricultural Library, Beltsville, Maryland, U.S.A.
19. Bill MacLennan, Reference Services, Canadian Agriculture

Library, Ottawa, Ontario, Canada.

20. S.R. Pietropaoli, Commander, U.S. Navy Assistant Chief of Information (media Operations), Navy Pentagon, Washington, D.C., U.S.A.

21. Brien Garnand, Archivist, The National PTA, Chicago, Illinois, U.S.A.

22. Arlene Morrison, Alexander Graham Bell Club, Baddeck, Nova Scotia, Canada.

23. Greater Richmond Chamber of Commerce, Richmond, Virginia, U.S.A.

24. Diana Holloway, Hampton Roads Chamber of Commerce, Norfolk, Virginia, U.S.A.

25. Ben Steinberg, Reference Department, Cambridge Public Library, Cambridge, Massachusetts, U.S.A.

26. Virginia McHugh, Executive Director, Association Montessori International (AMI-USA), New York, U.S.A.

27. Margaret M. Keir, Head Teacher, Garvel Deaf Centre, Greenock, Scotland.

28. Judy Lawry Ball, Photo Researcher, Capital Images Inc. Potomac, Maryland, U.S.A.

Very special thanks to my parents, Eve and Steve Batty, who always encouraged me to follow my heart, to my daughters Beverlee (thanks for all your computer expertise Bev!), Stephanie, Jaclyn and Samantha for their patience over the past several years and who could always make me smile when things got tough.

Thank you also to the following for their support , help and encouragement:-

CBC Radio "Information Morning", Sydney, Nova Scotia, Canada
        (Aileen Rudderham)

Boston Sunday Herald, Boston, Massachusetts, U.S.A.

Cape Breton Post, Canada

Montreal Gazette (Women's News), Canada

Greenock Telegraph, Scotland

Quebec Federation of Home & Schools Association (QFHSA)
        Montreal, Quebec, Canada
        (Donna Sauriol, Wendy Buchanan, Pat Waters, Barbara
        Milne-Smith & Carol Ohlin)

Canadian Home & School Federation (CHSF)

Studio Melrose, Montreal – Ted Sancton

- and my friends, Cher Jacek-Cote, Cathy Bridgeman, Joan Newsome, and Raizel Candib

Peggy Wadsworth - thanks for telling me about the Mabel Hubbard Club!

All the teaching staff at Elizabeth Ballantyne School, Montreal West

Librarian, Karen Findlay, Royal West Academy, Montreal West

Printed in the United States
5328